HOW TO DRAW EMOJIS

for Kids, Teens and Adults

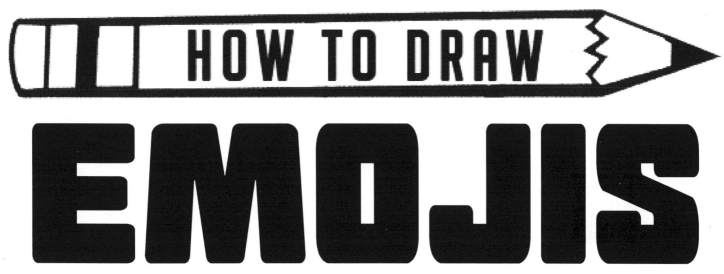

EMOJILIFE COLORING

1

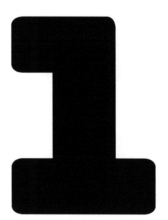

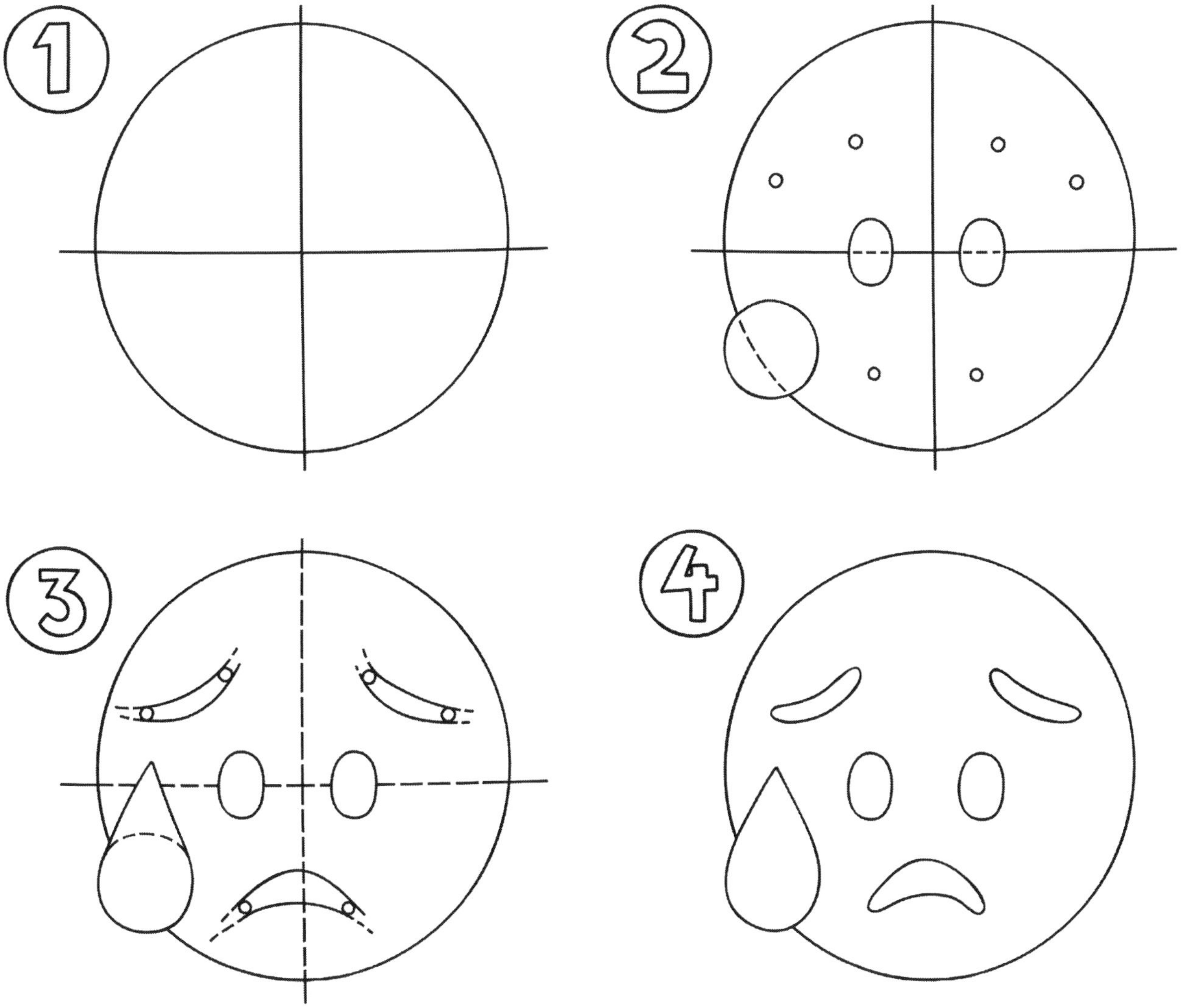
1
2
3
4

YOU TRY

2

1
2
3
4

YOU TRY

3

1
2
3
4
YOU DRAW

4

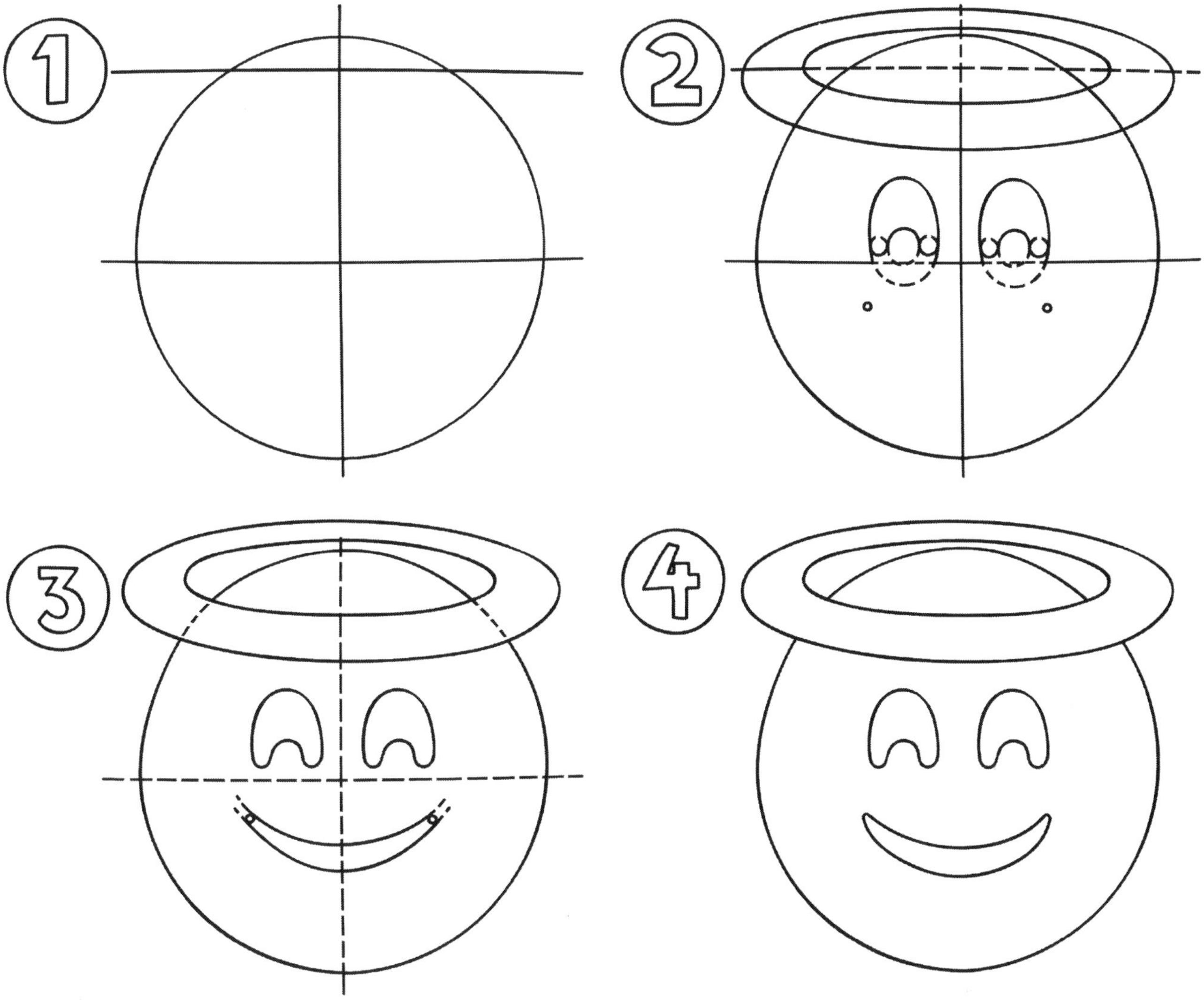
1
2
3
4

YOU TRY

5

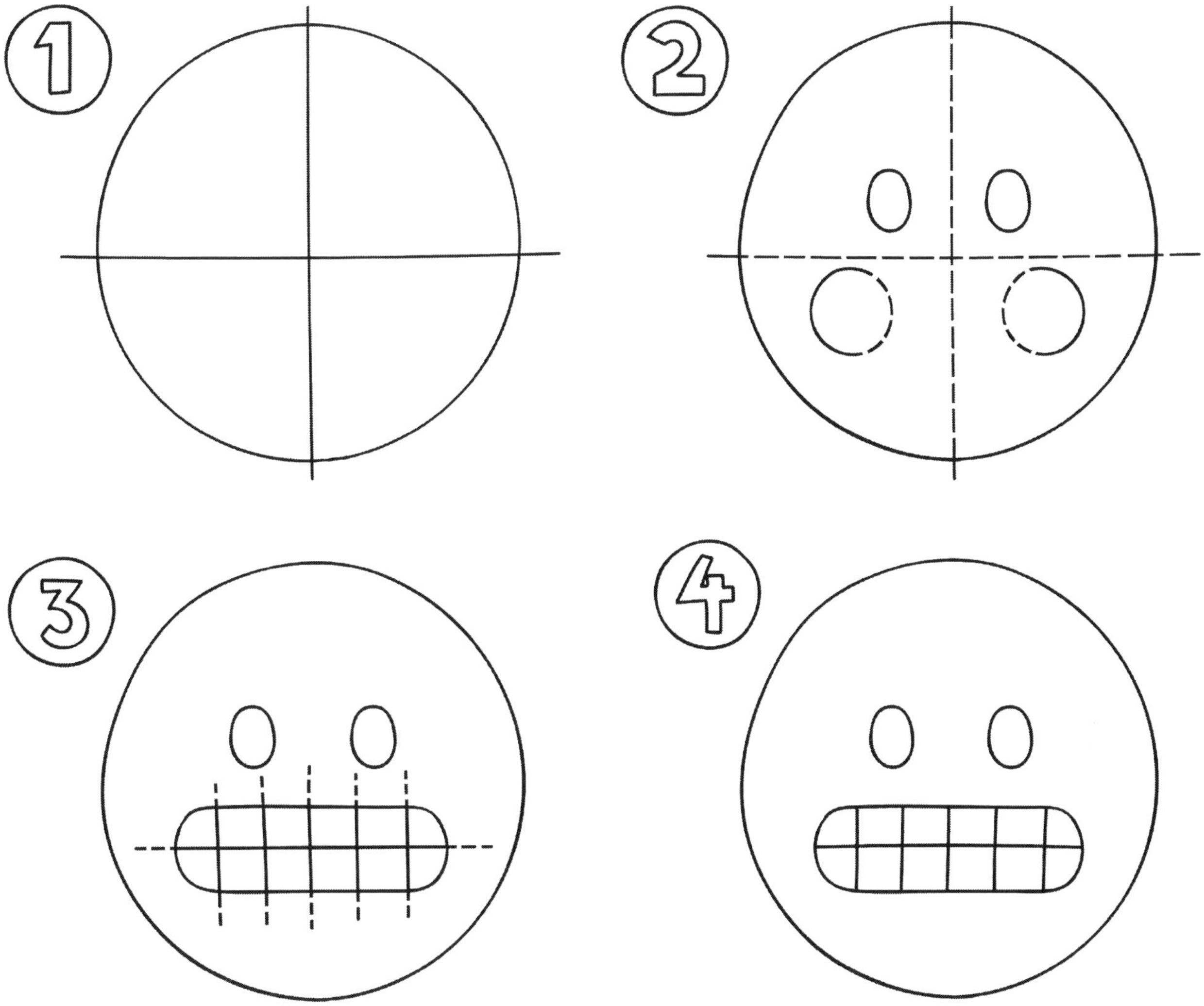
1
2
3
4

YOU TRY

6

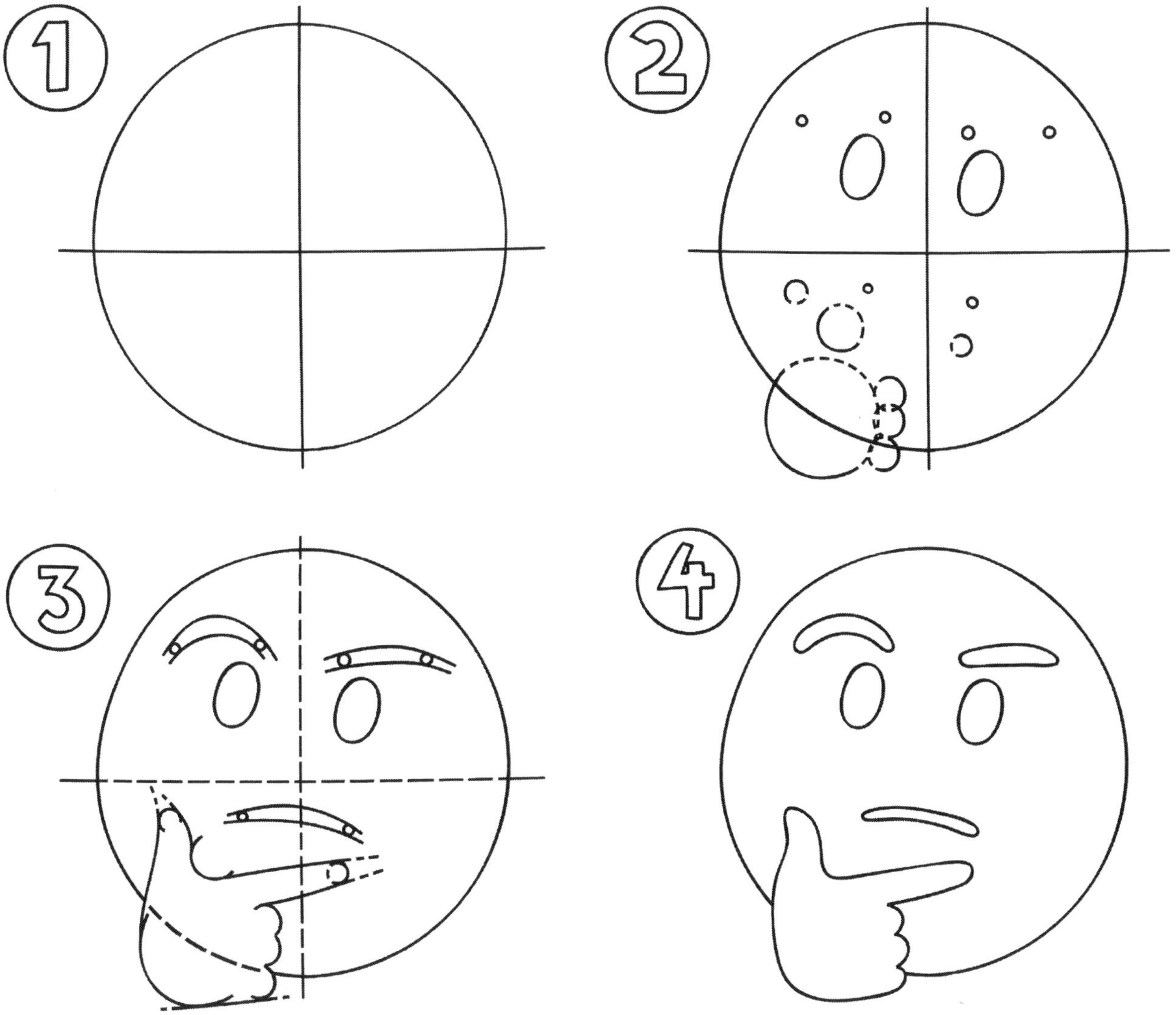
1
2
3
4

YOU TRY

7

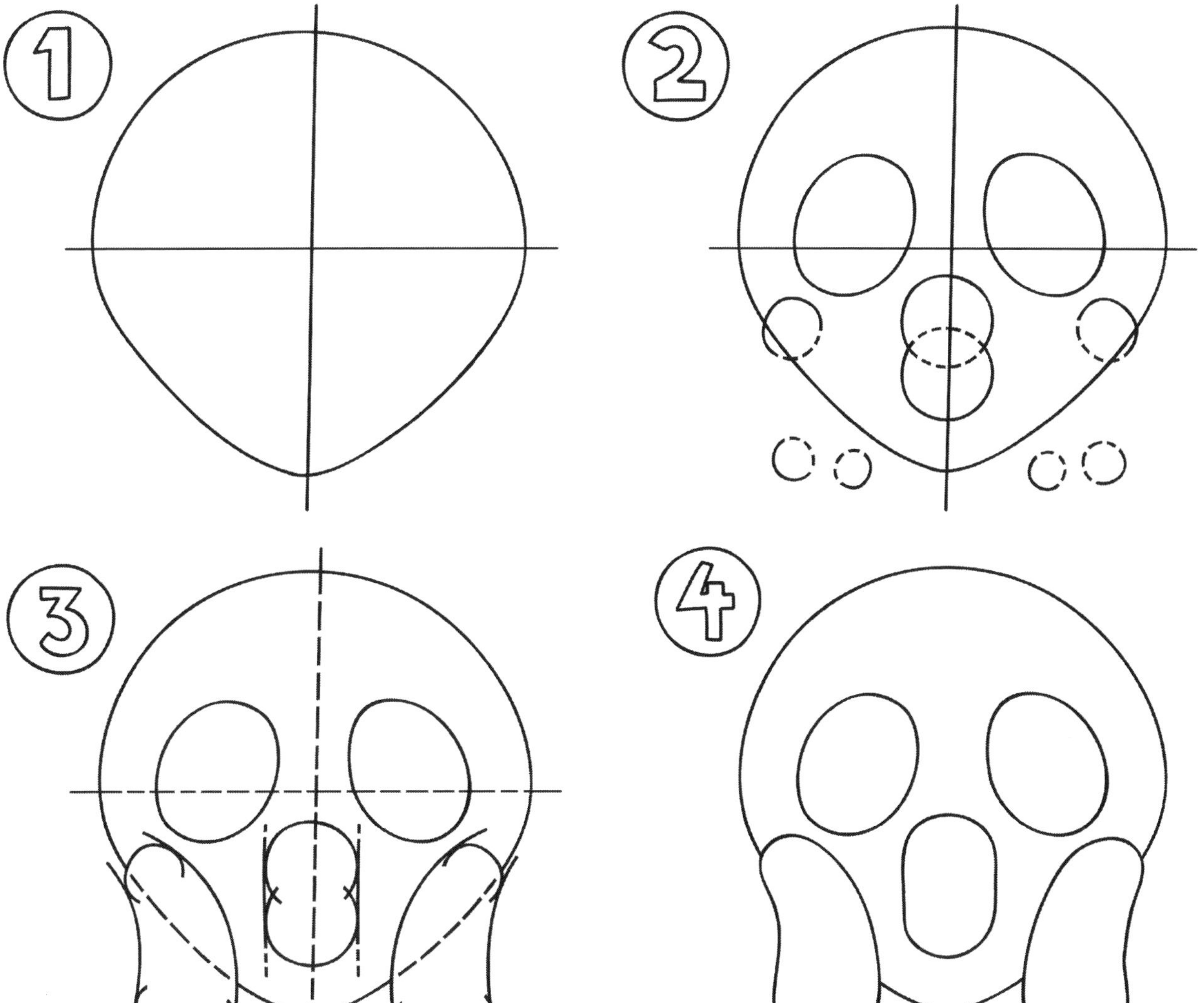
1
2
3
4

YOU TRY

8

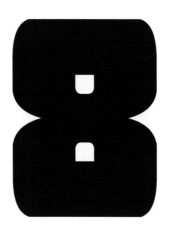

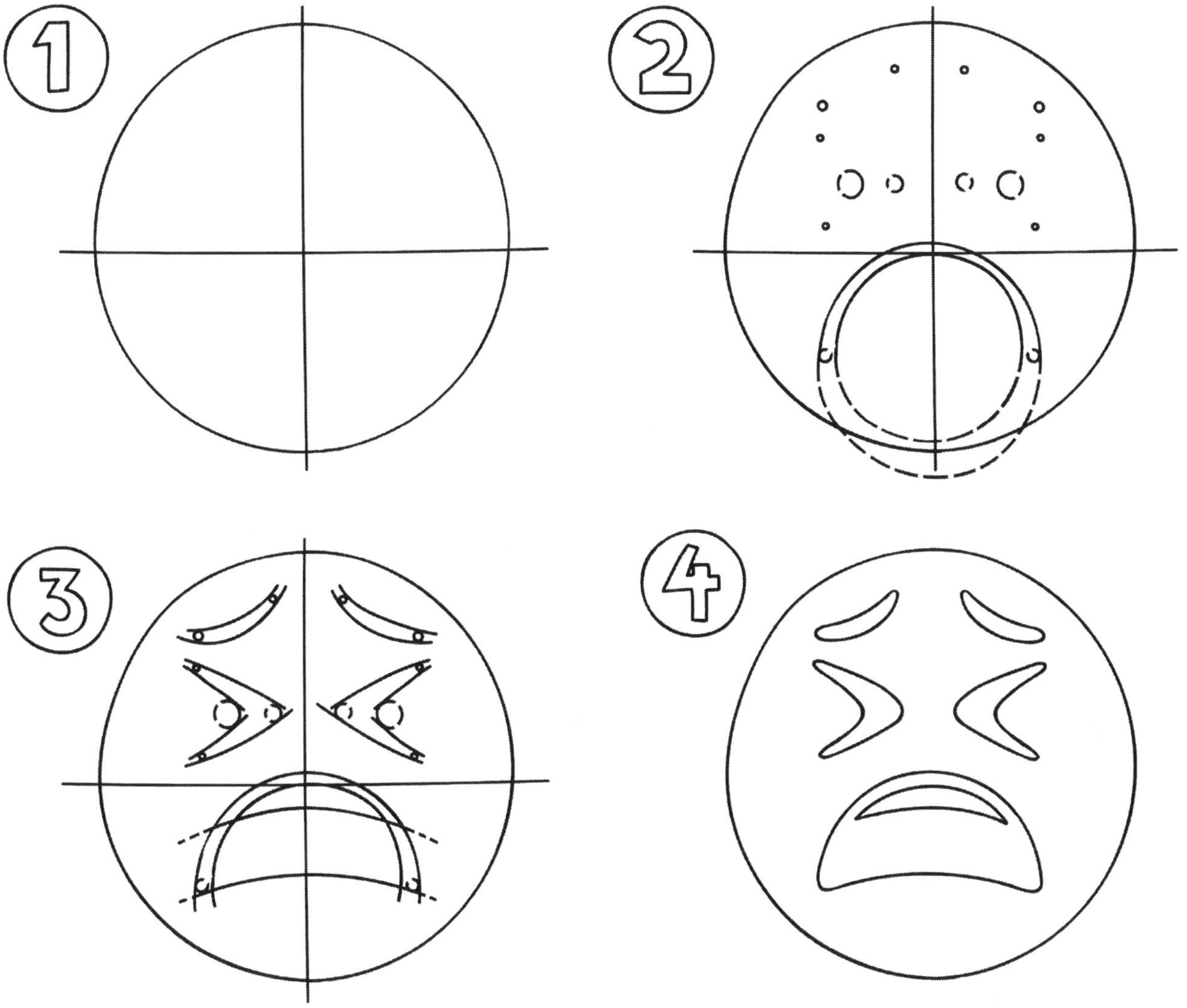
1
2
3
4

YOU TRY

9

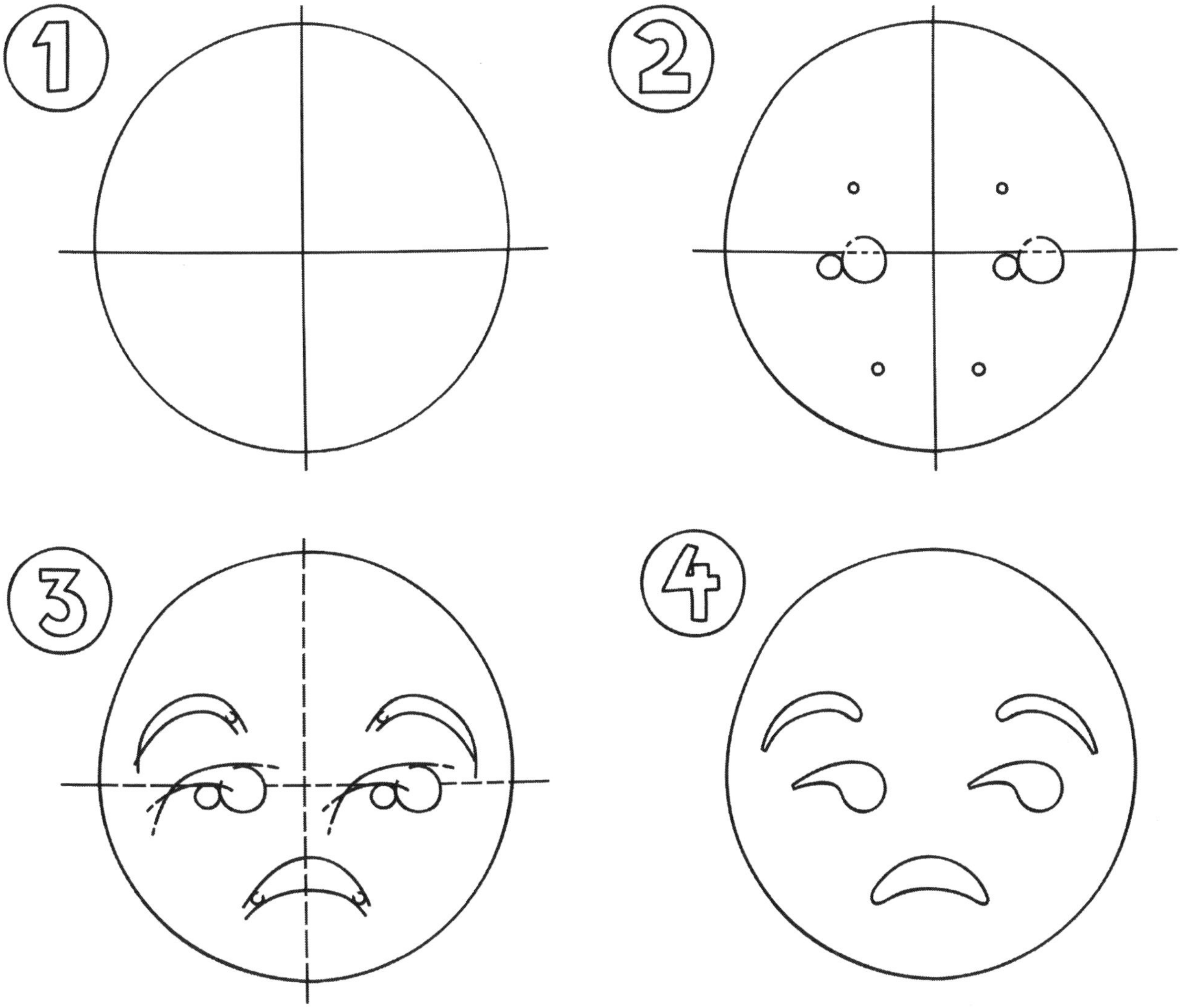
1
2
3
4

YOU TRY

10

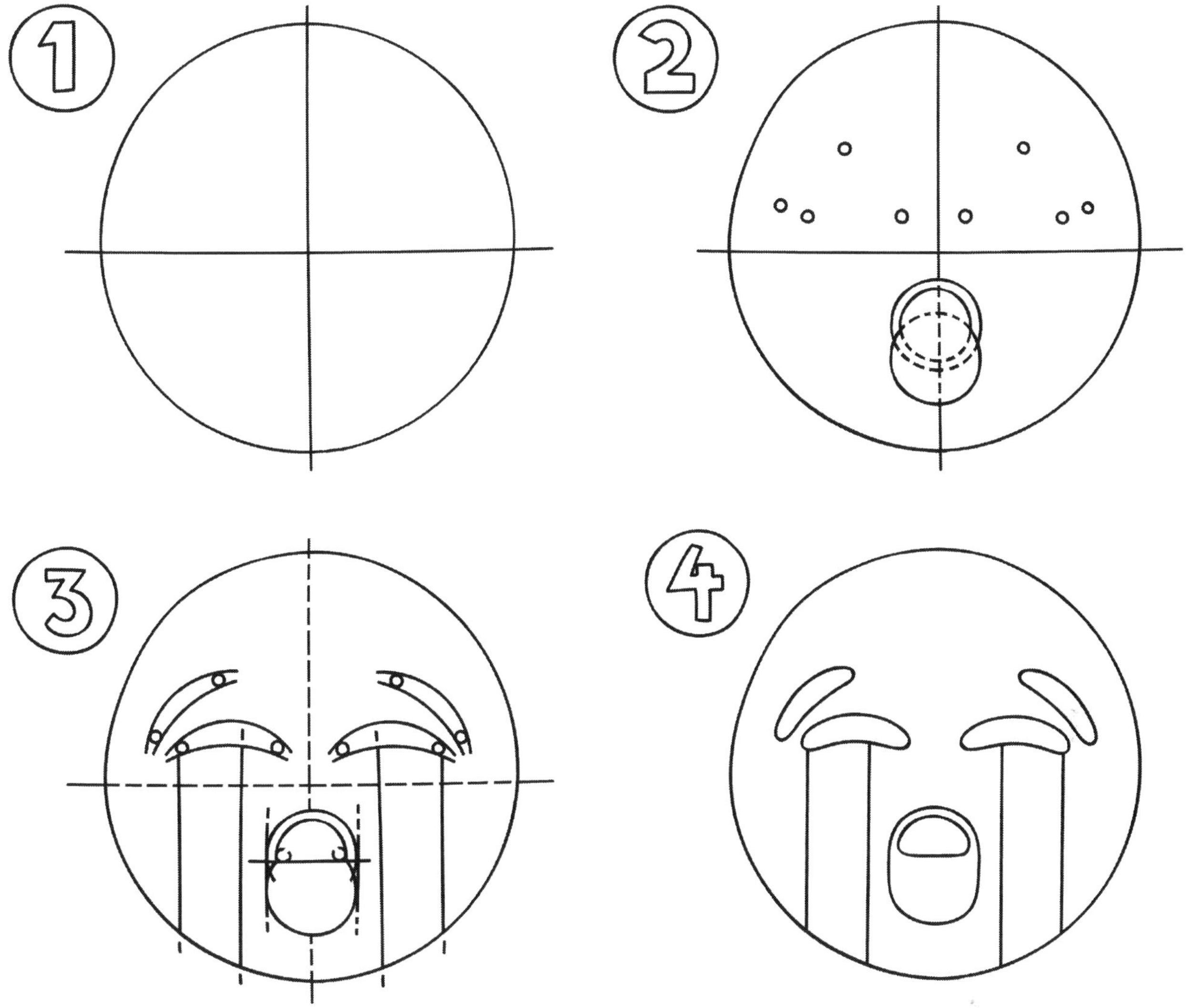
1
2
3
4

YOU TRY

11

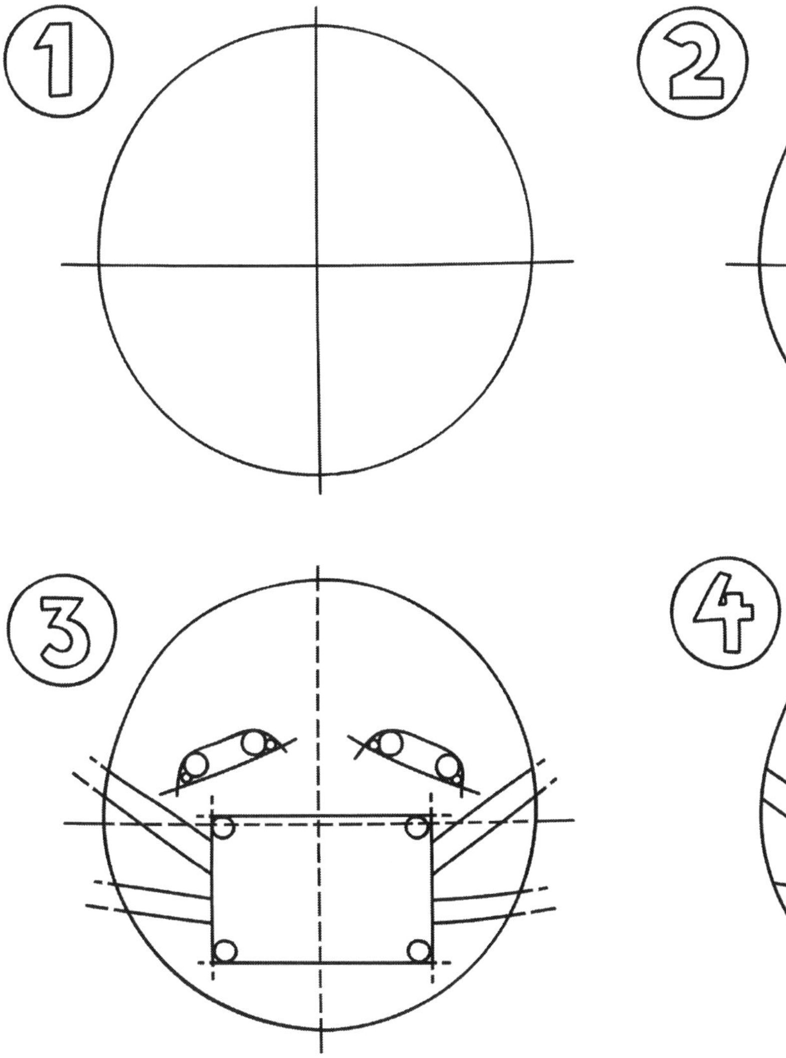
1
2
3
4

YOU TRY

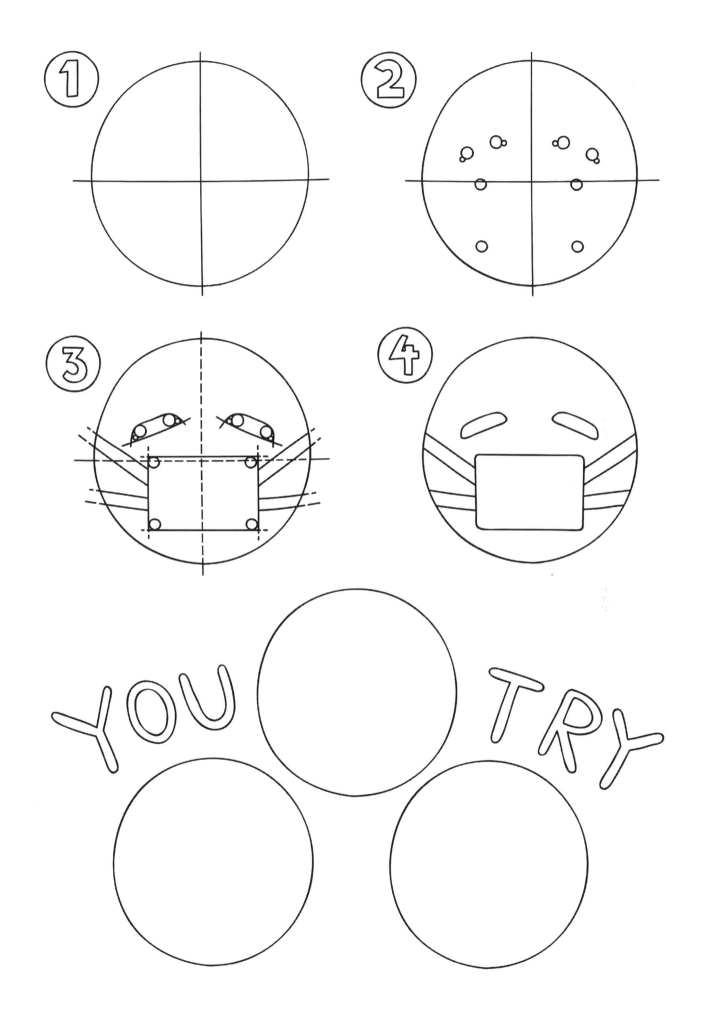

12

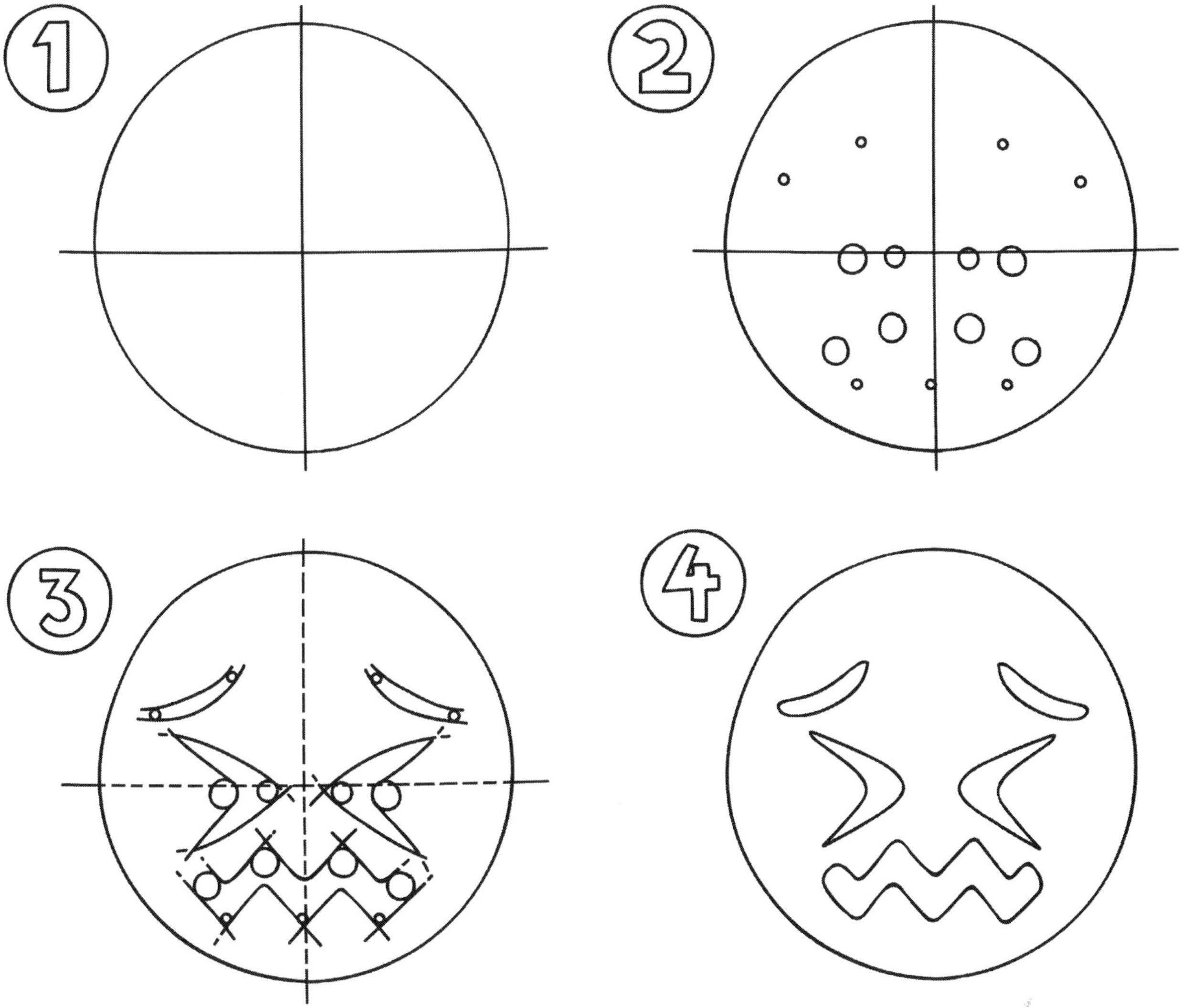
1
2
3
4

YOU TRY

13

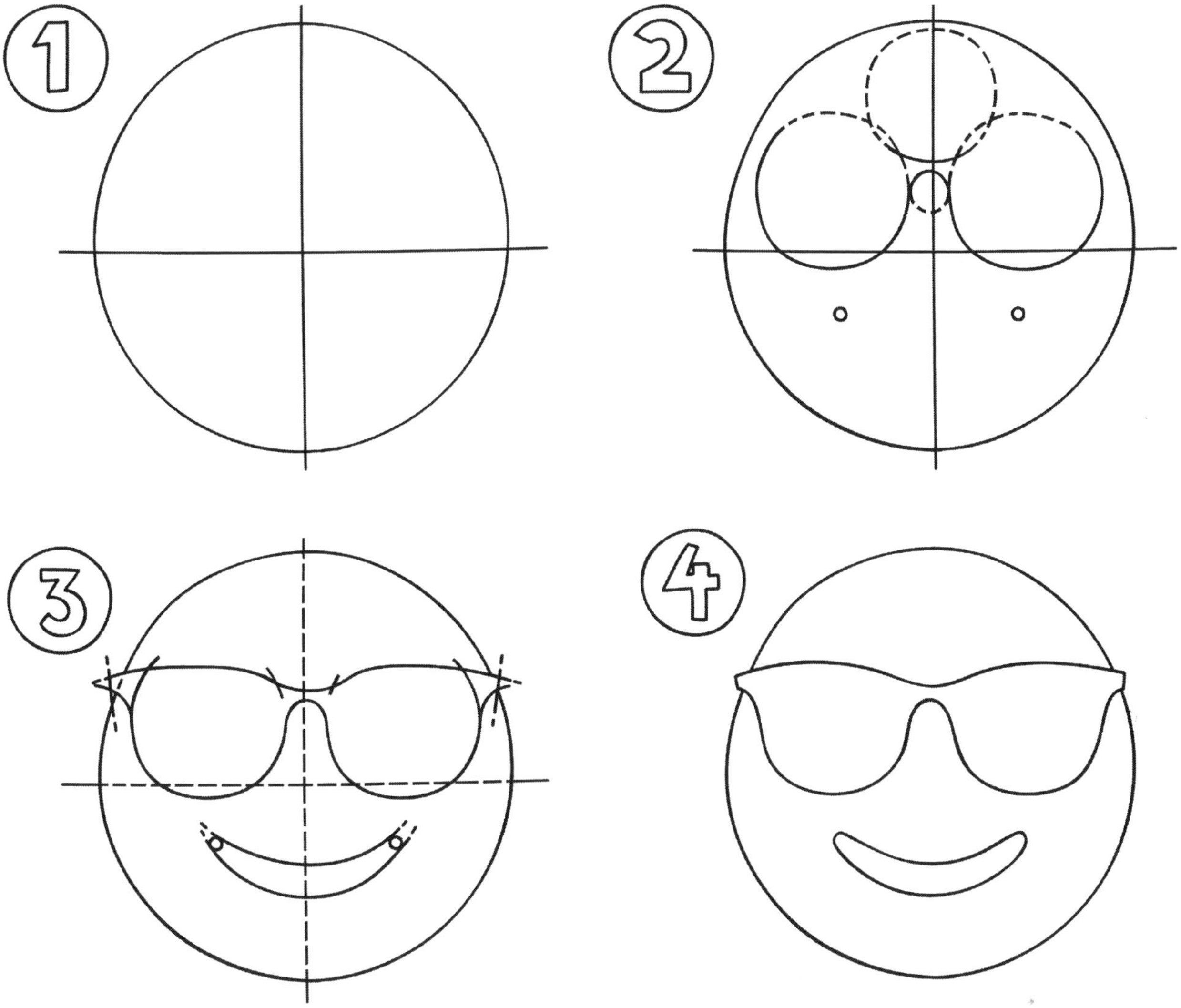
1
2
3
4

YOU TRY

14

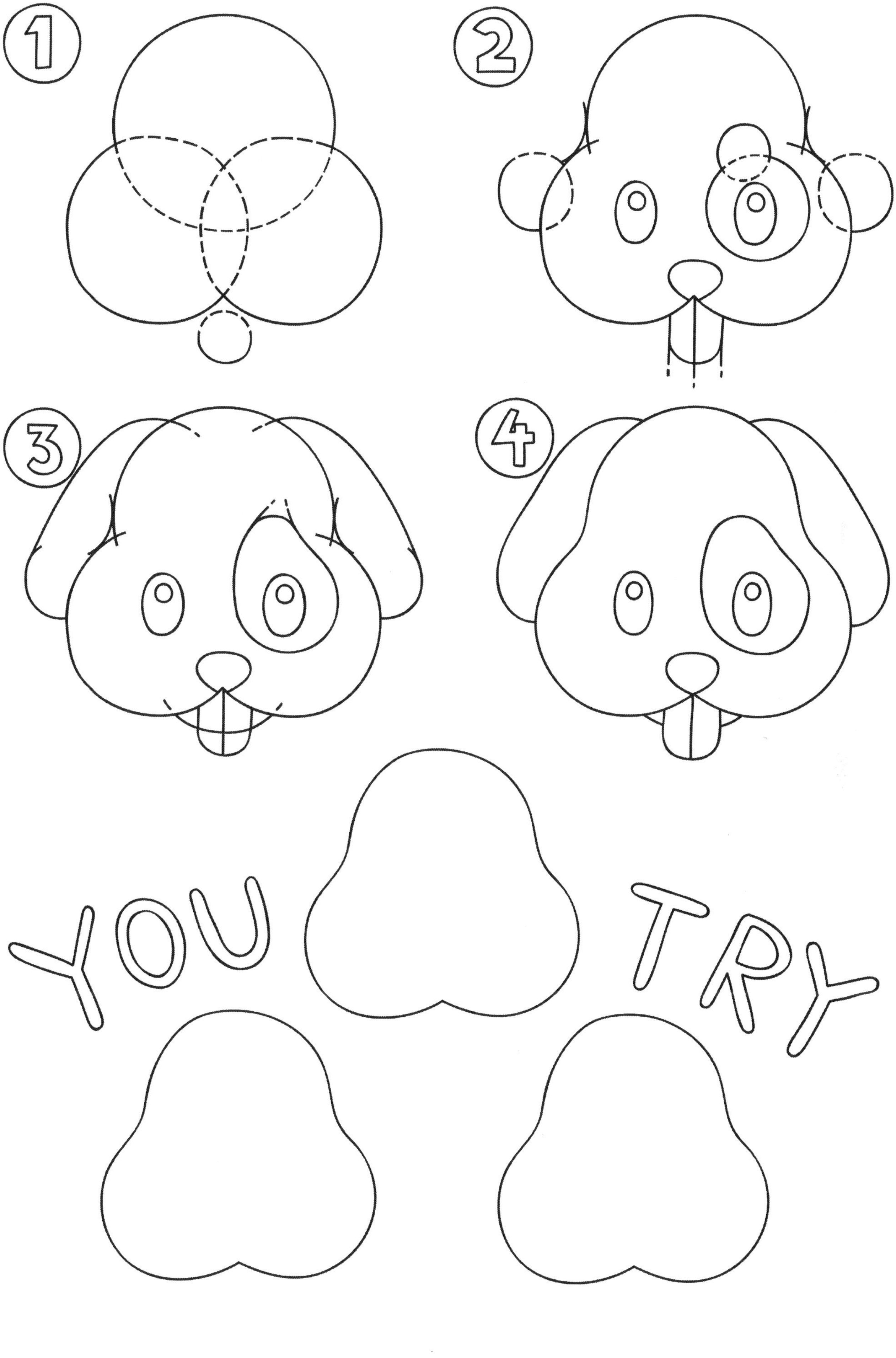
1
2
3
4
YOU TRY

15

1
2
3
4
YOU TRY

16

1

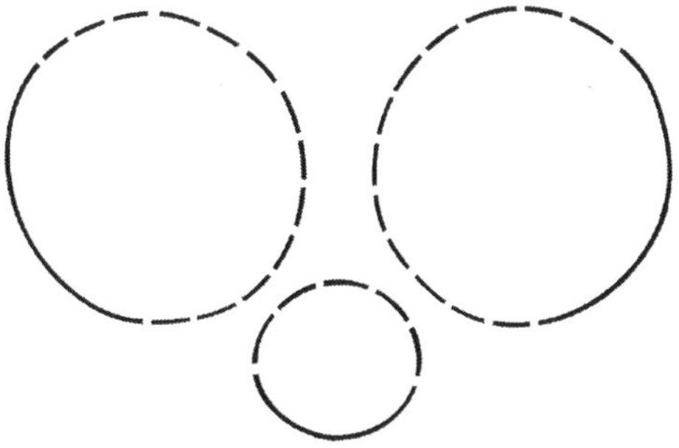

2

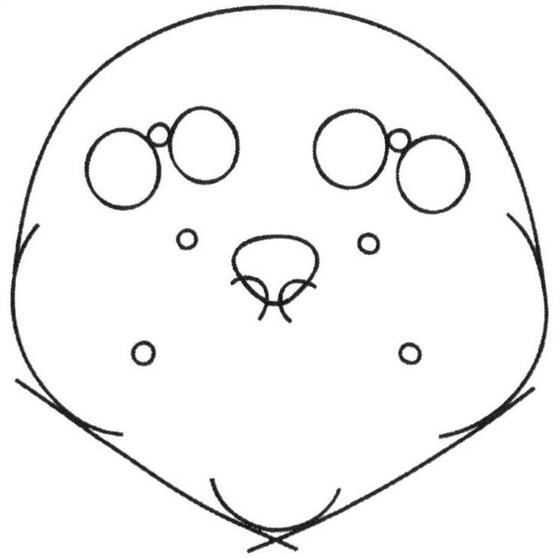

3

4

YOU

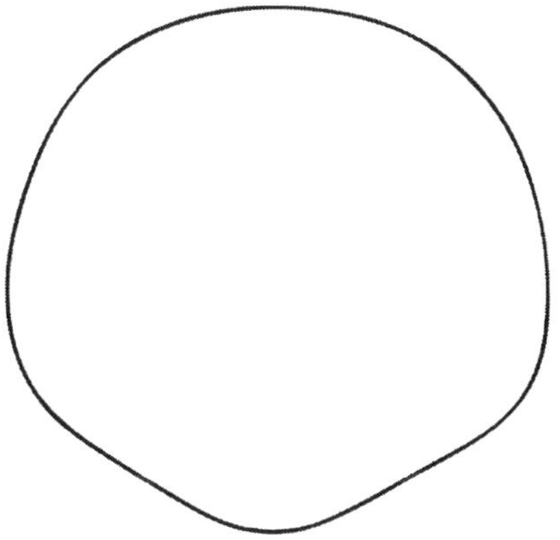

TRY

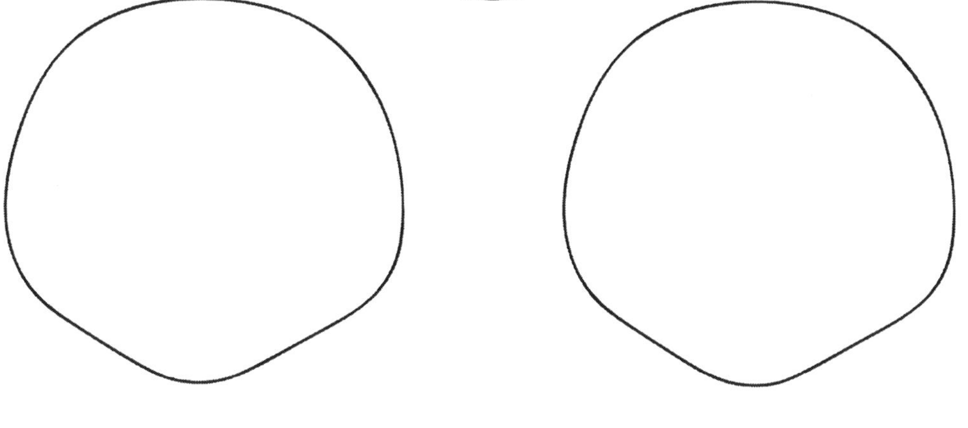

17

1
2
3
4

YOU TRY

18

1
2
3
4

YOU TRY

19

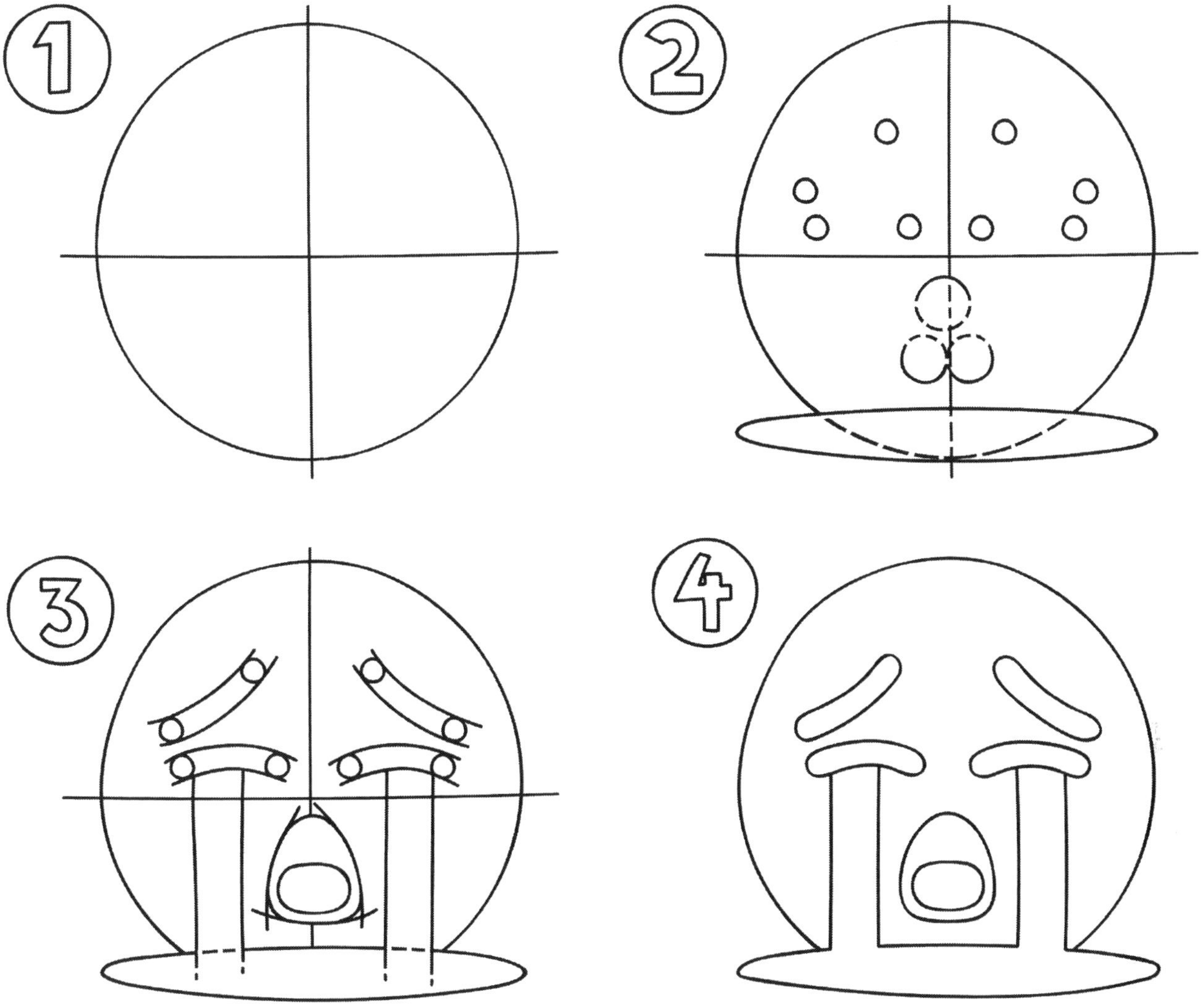
1
2
3
4

YOU TRY

20

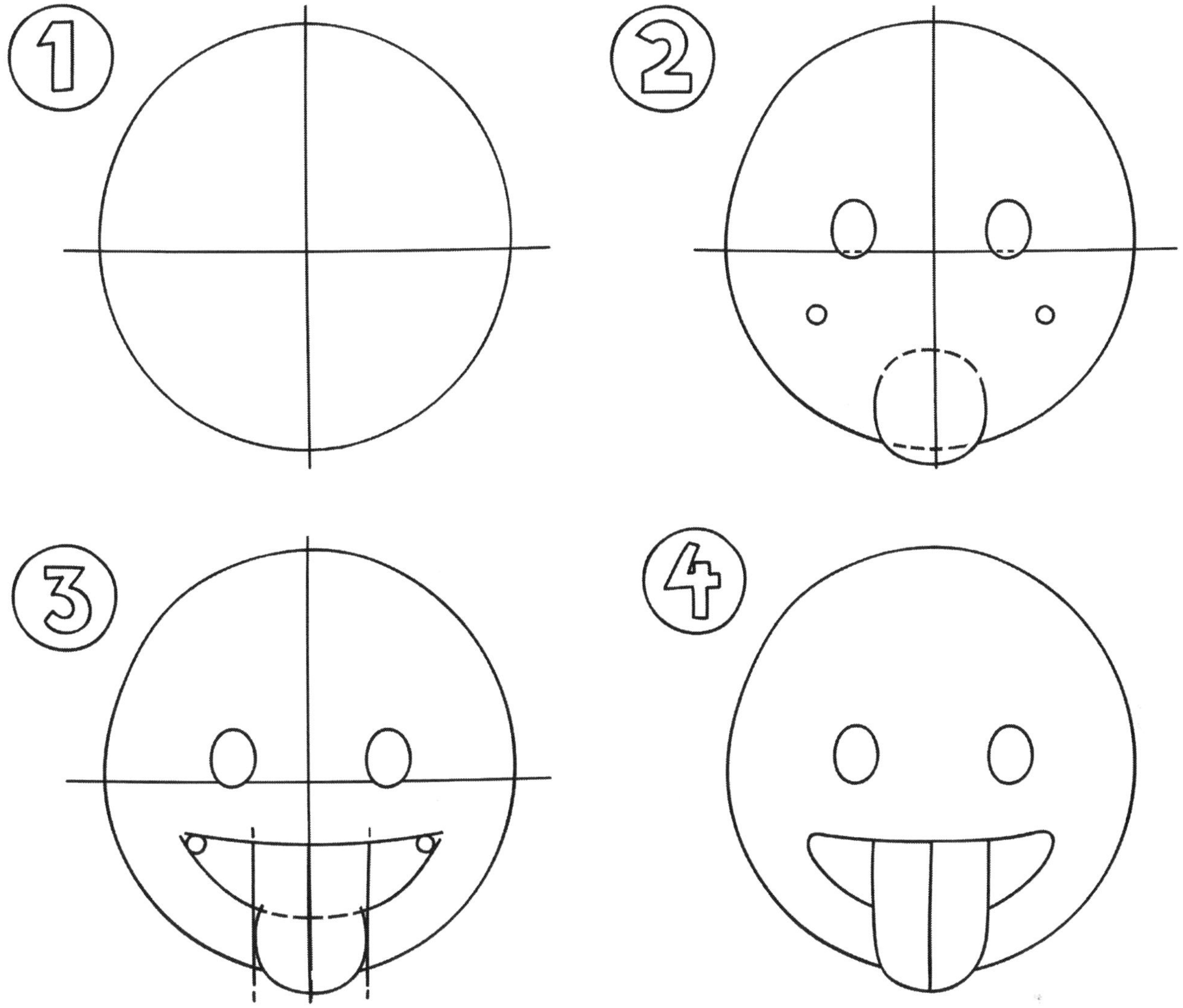
1
2
3
4

YOU TRY

21

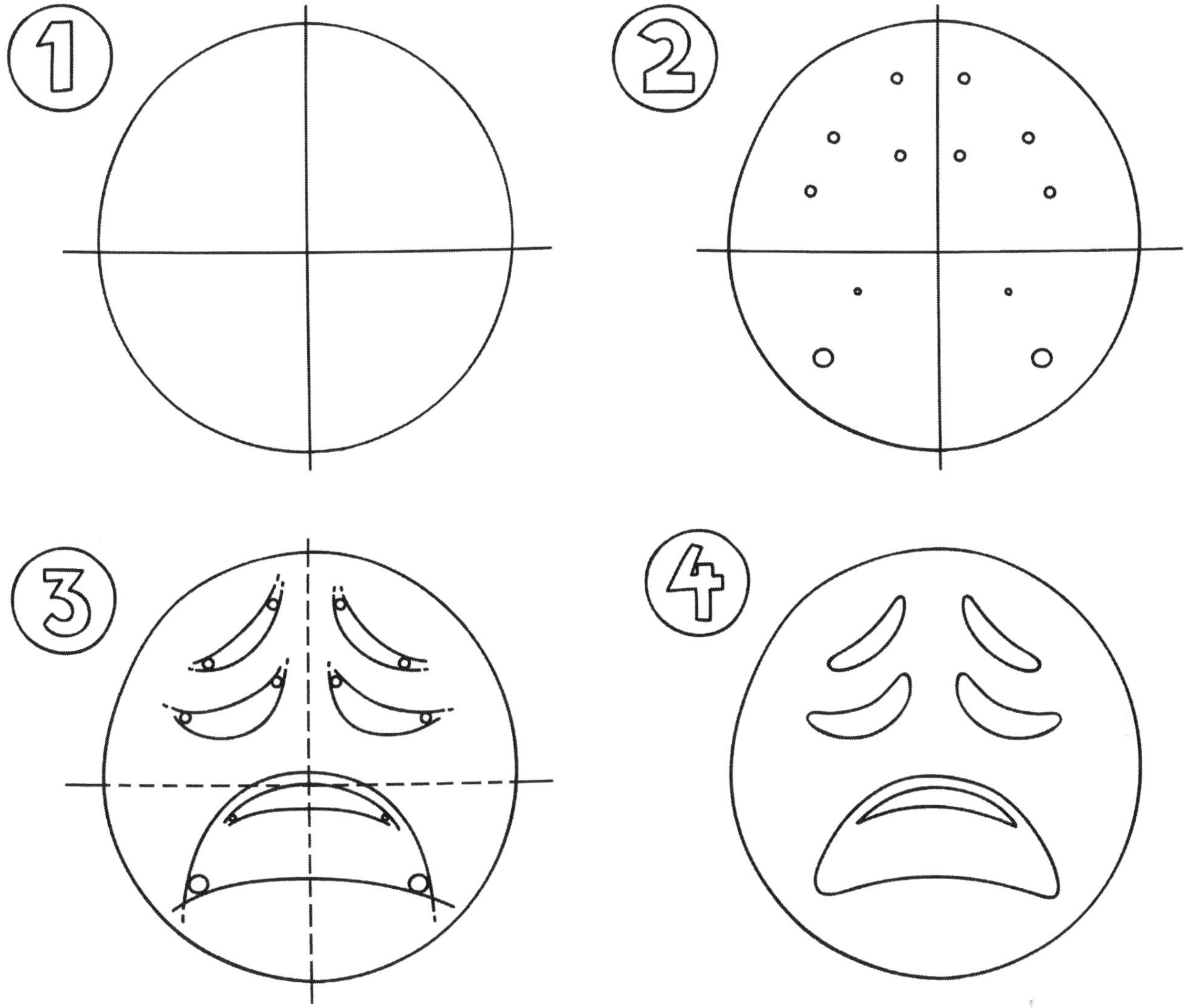
1
2
3
4

YOU TRY

22

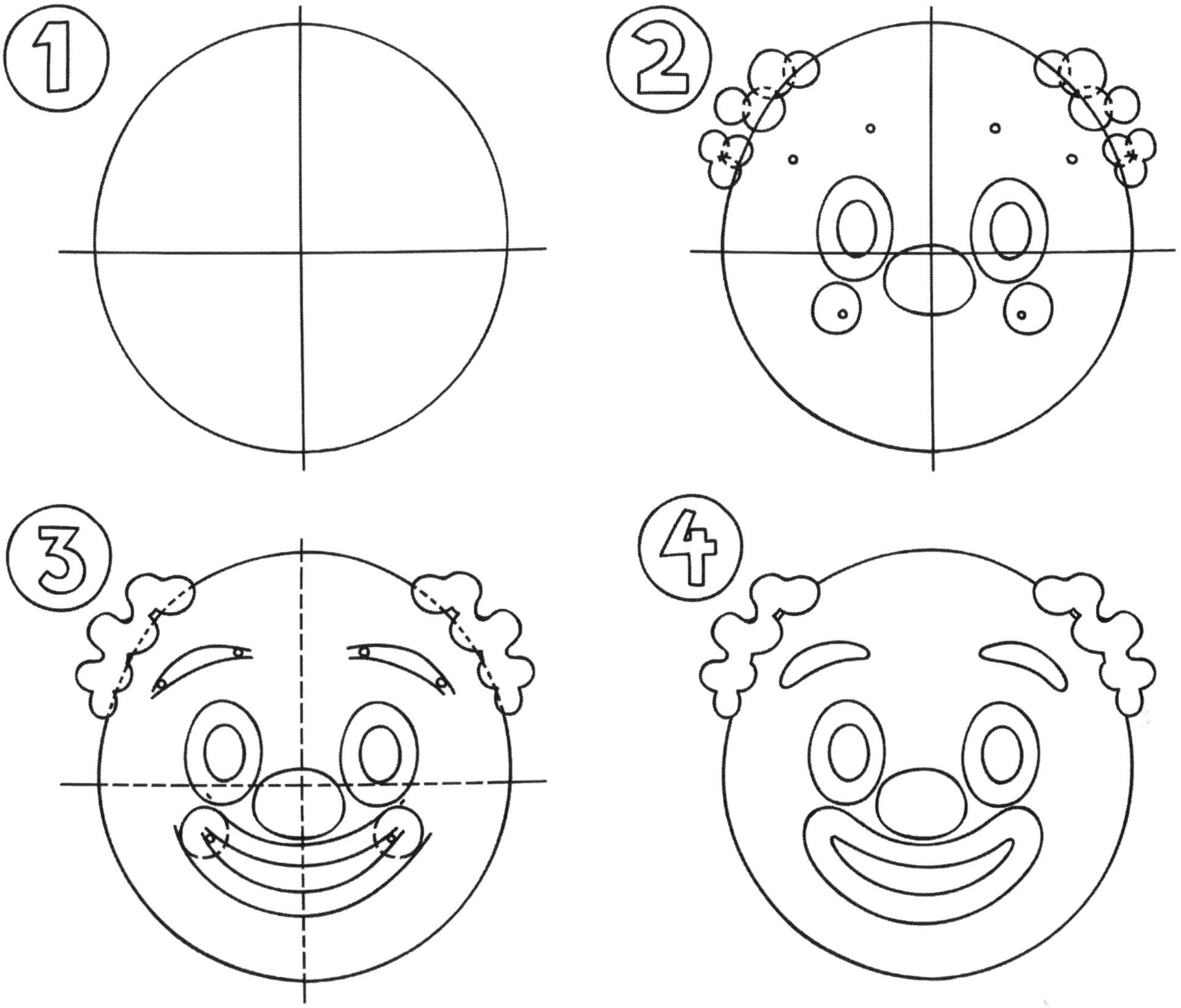
1
2
3
4

YOU TRY

23

1
2
3
4
YOU TRY

24

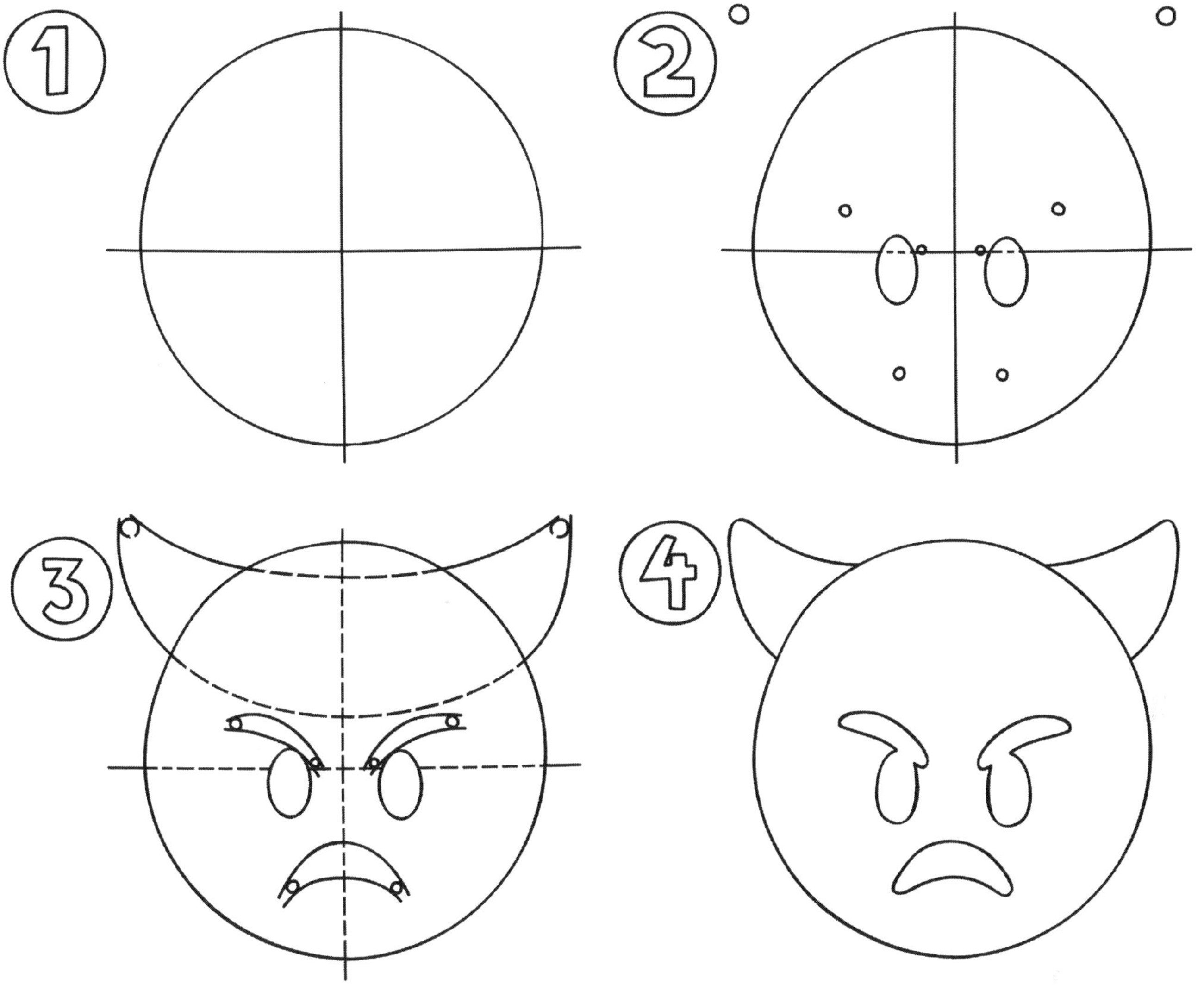
1
2
3
4

YOU TRY

25

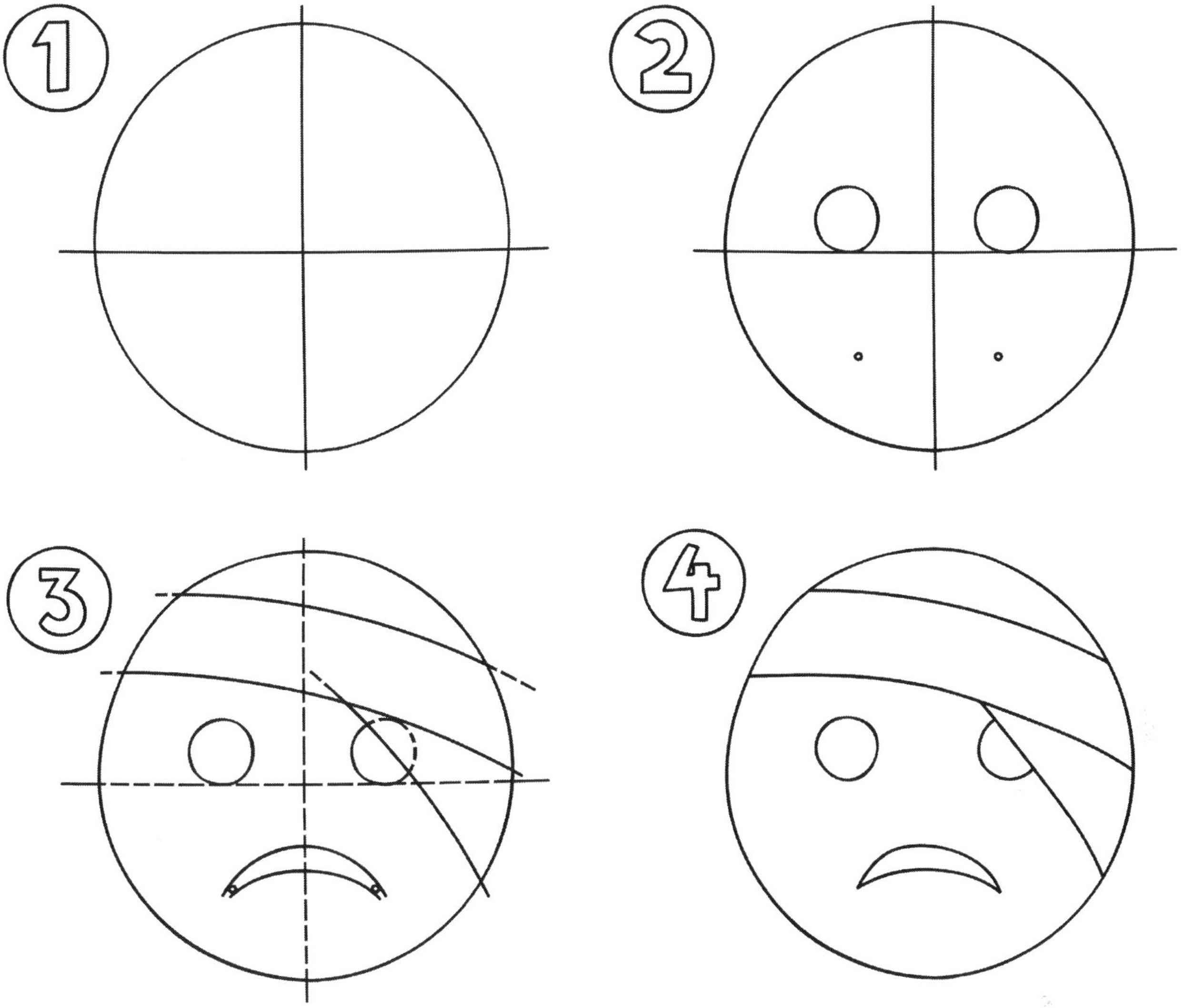
1
2
3
4

YOU TRY

26

1
2
3
4
YOU TRY

27

1
2
3
4

YOU TRY

28

1

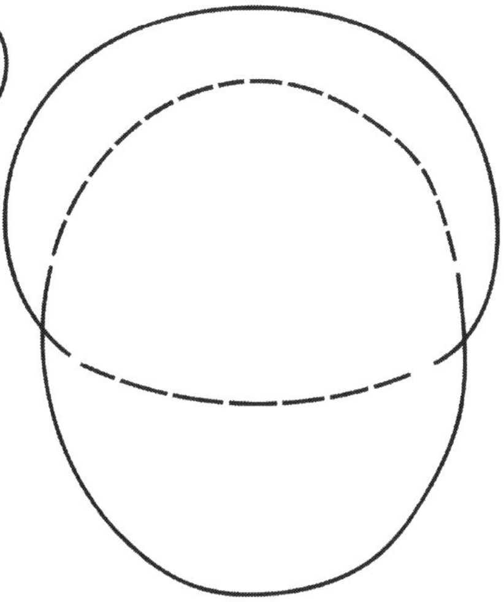

2

3

4

29

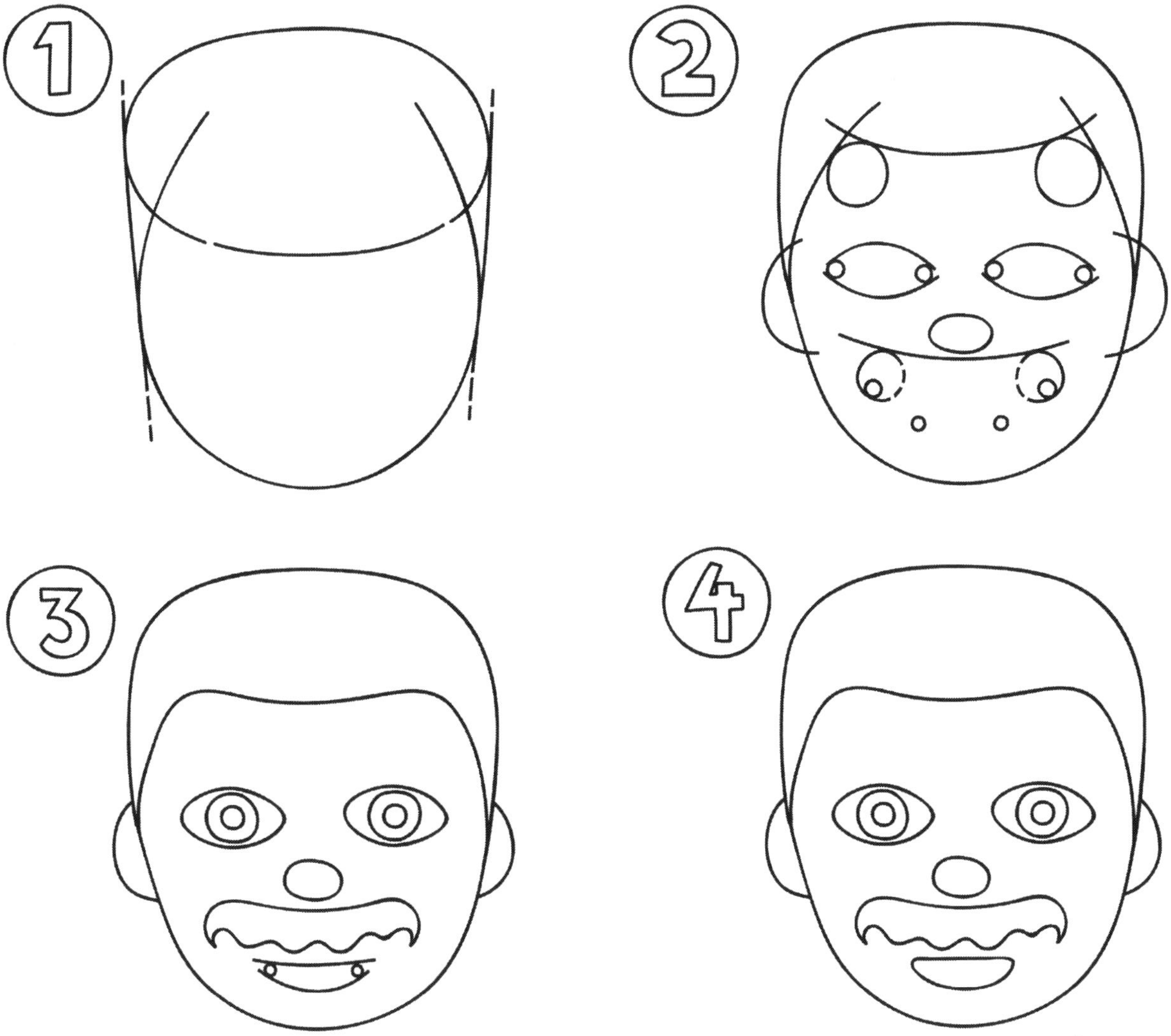
1
2
3
4

YOU TRY

30

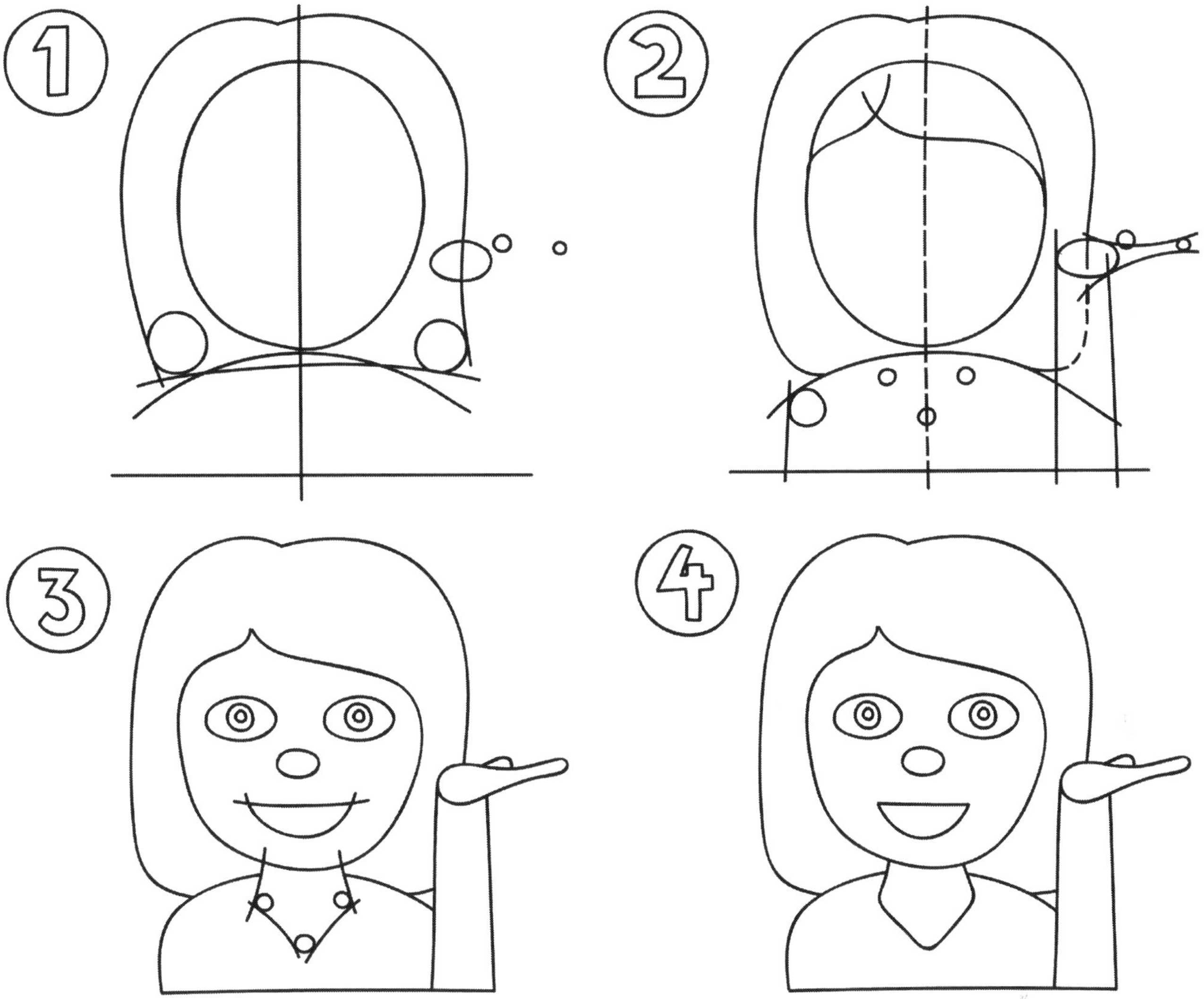

YOU TRY

31

YOU TRY

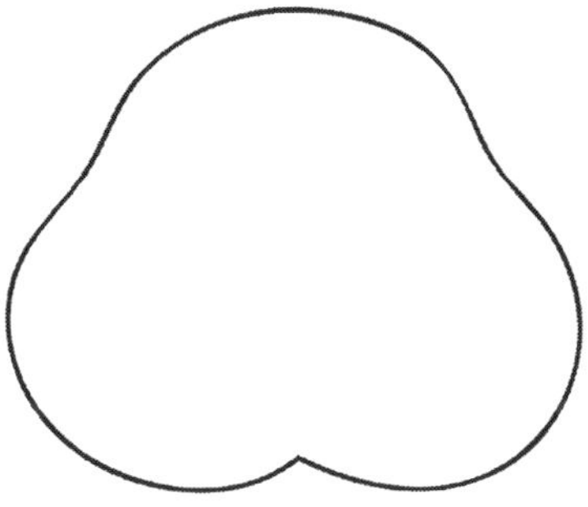

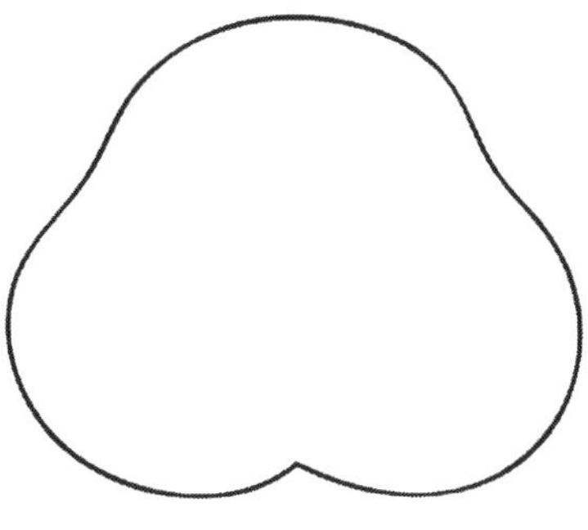

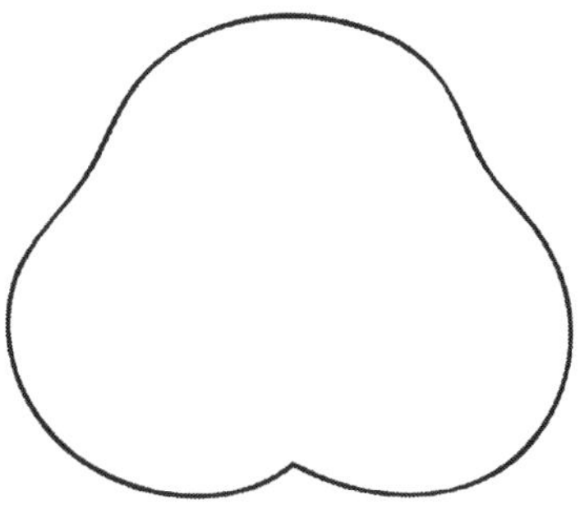

32

1
2
3
4

YOU TRY

33

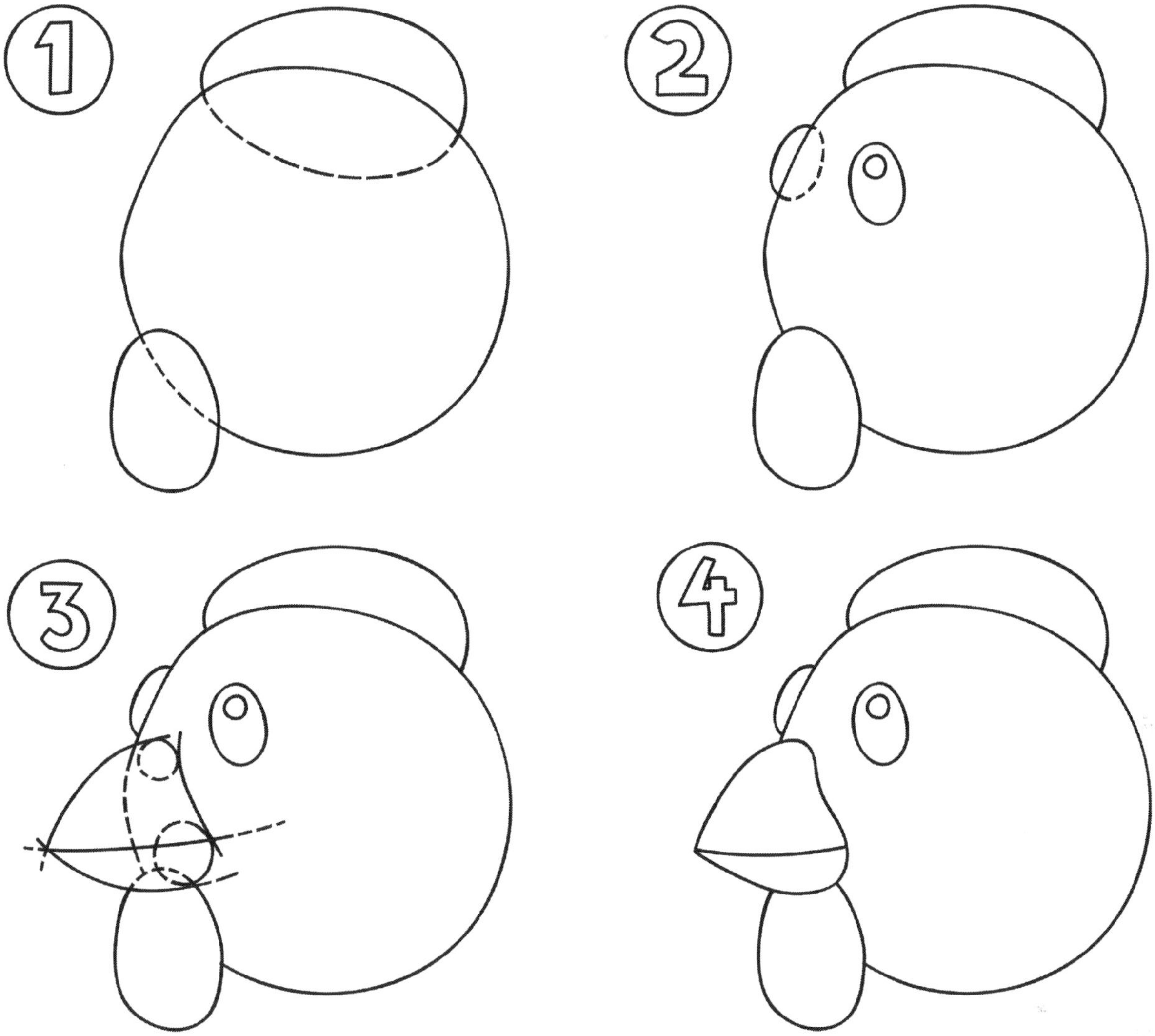
1
2
3
4

YOU TRY

34

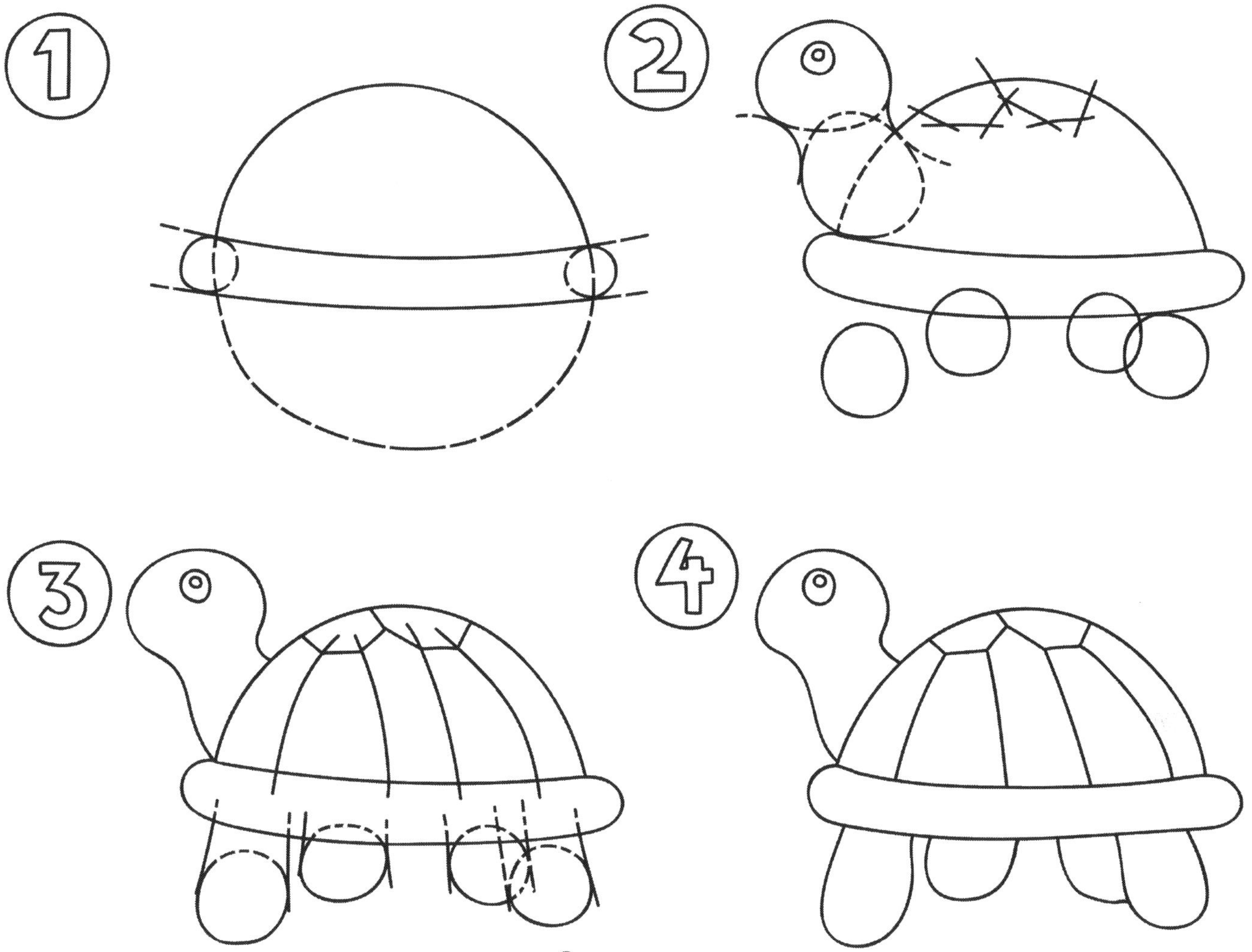

YOU TRY

35

YOU TRY

36

1
2
3
4

YOU TRY

37

1
2
3
4
YOU TRY

38

YOU TRY

39

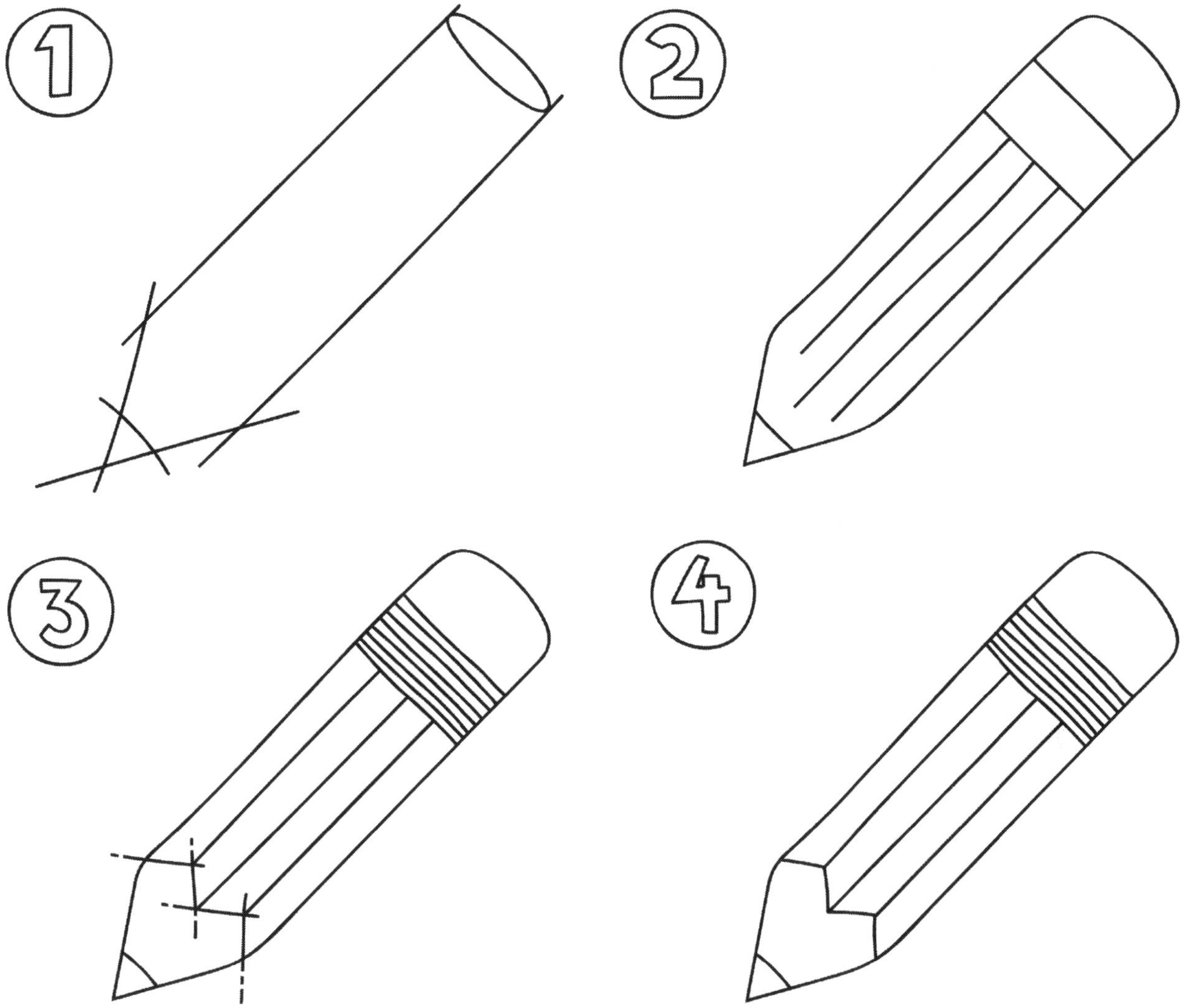

YOU TRY

40

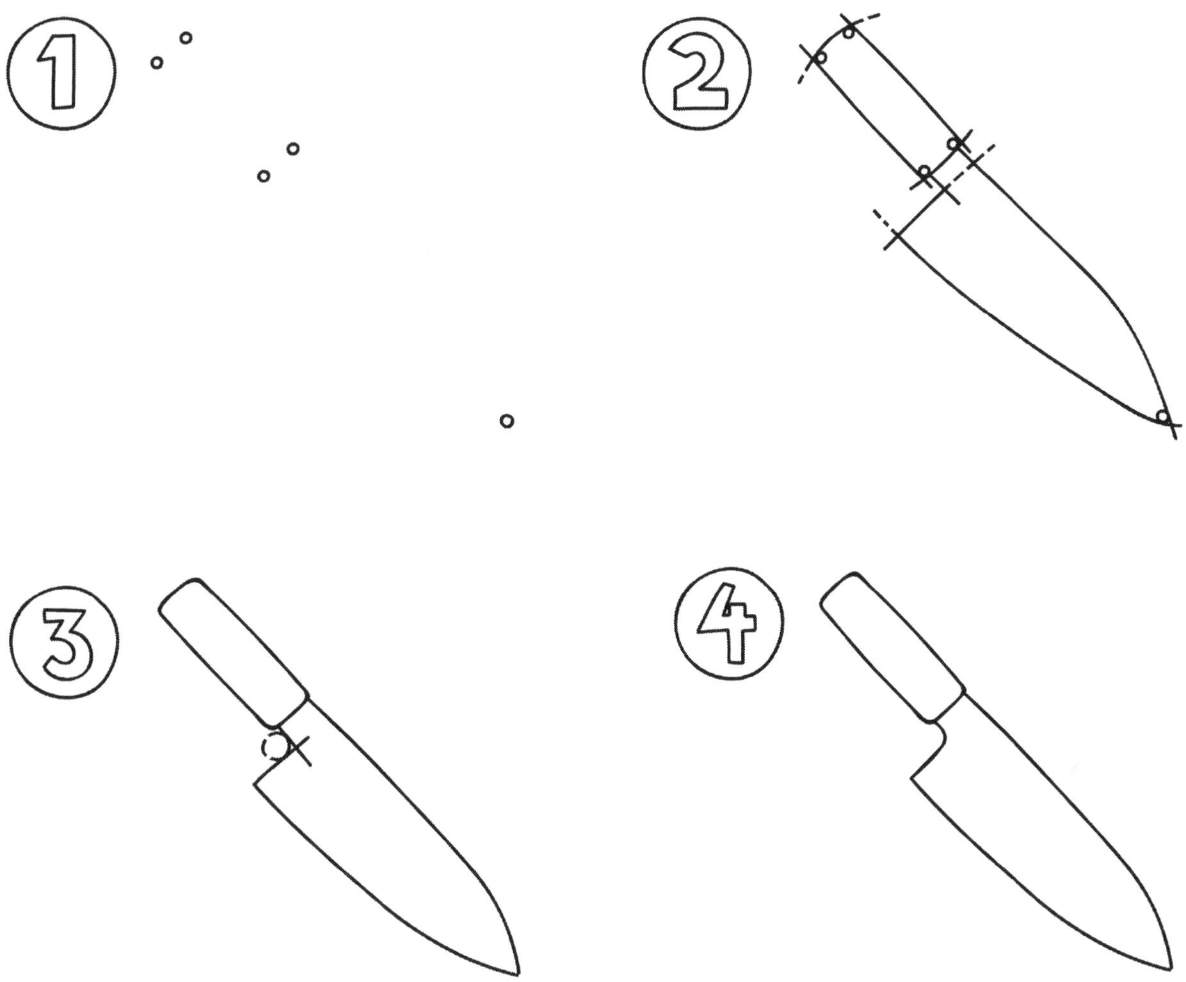

YOU TRY

41

1
2
3
4
YOU TRY

42

YOU TRY

43

1
2
3
4
YOU TRY

44

YOU TRY

45

YOU TRY

46

YOU TRY

47

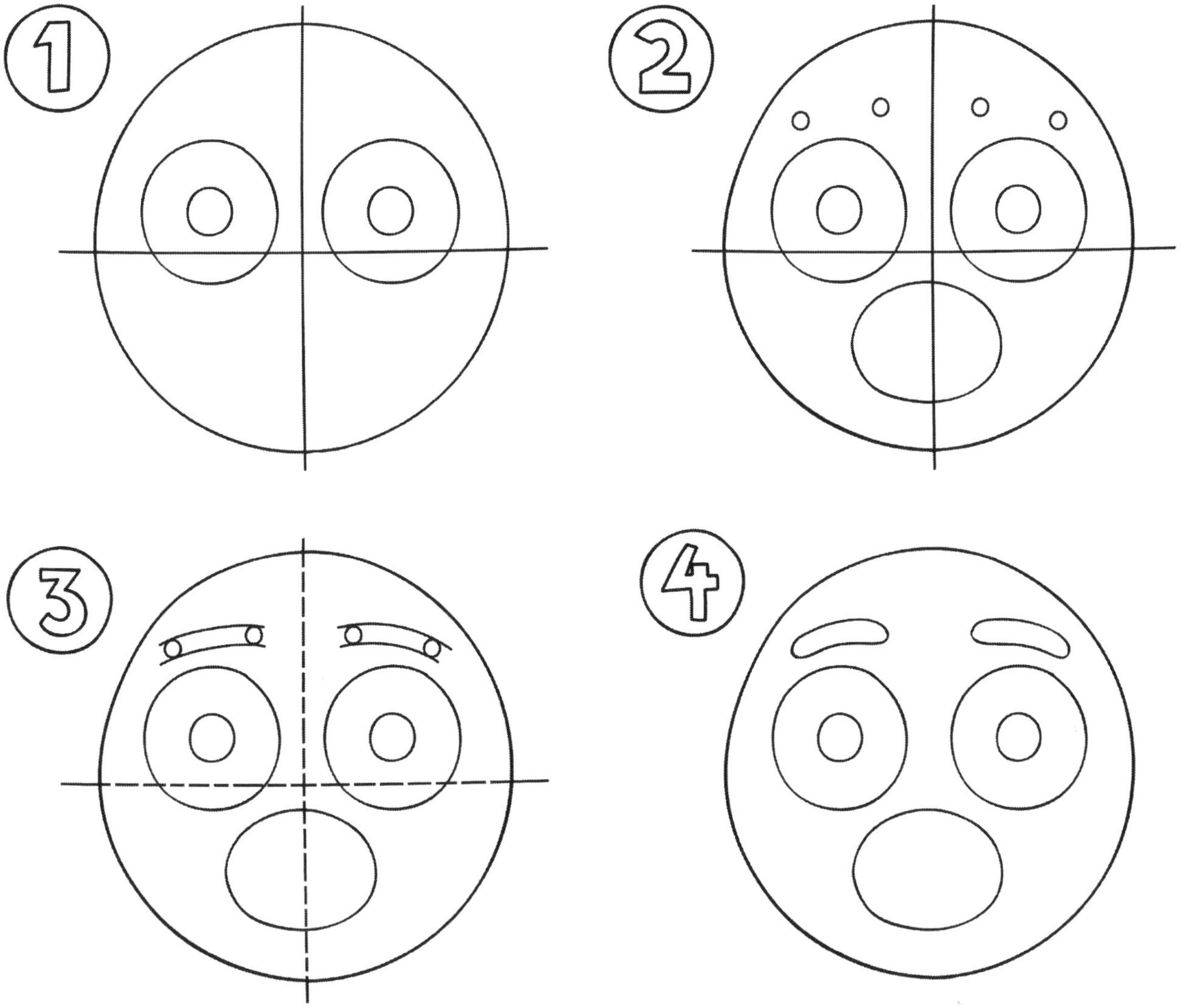
1
2
3
4

YOU TRY

48

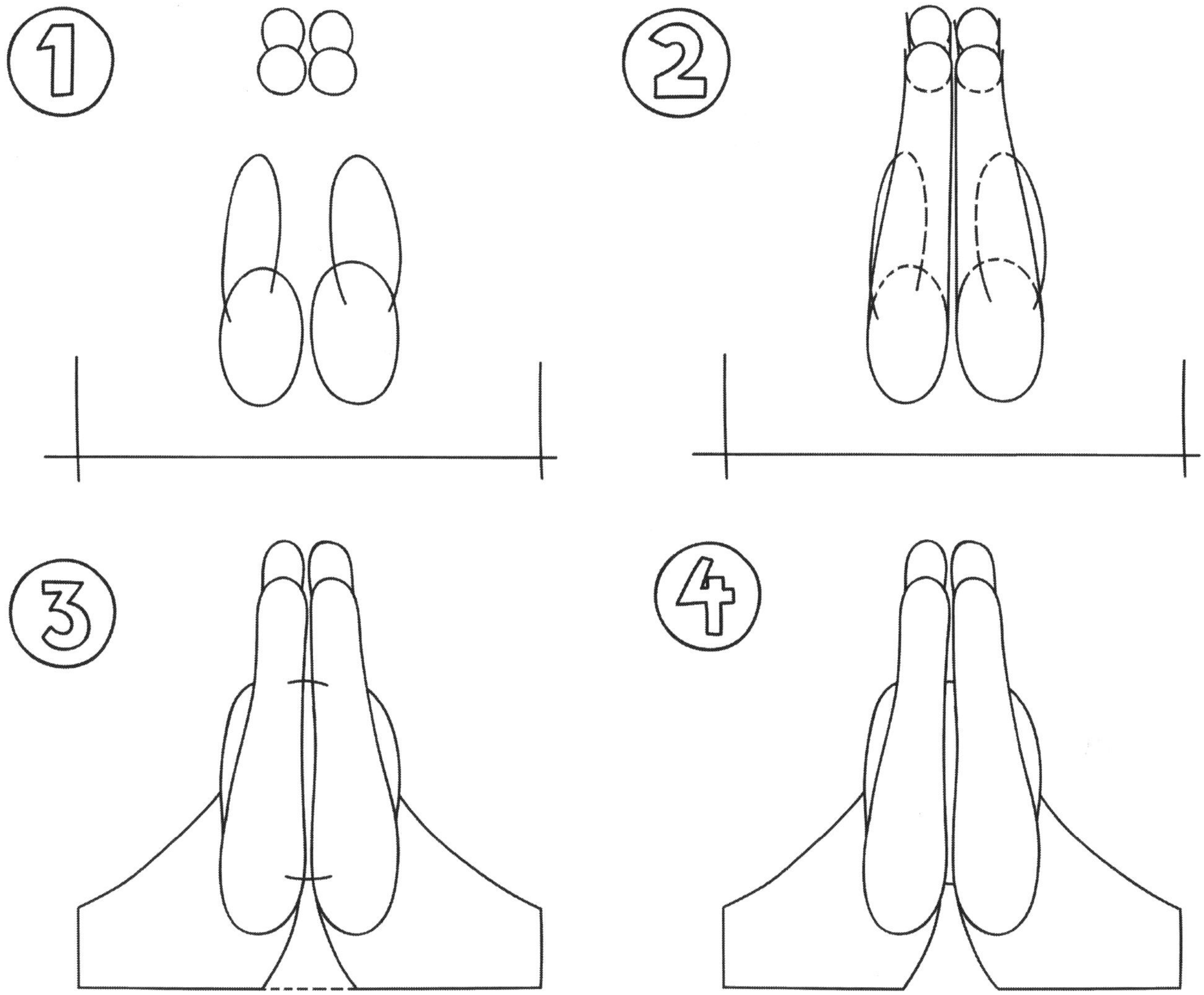

YOU TRY

49

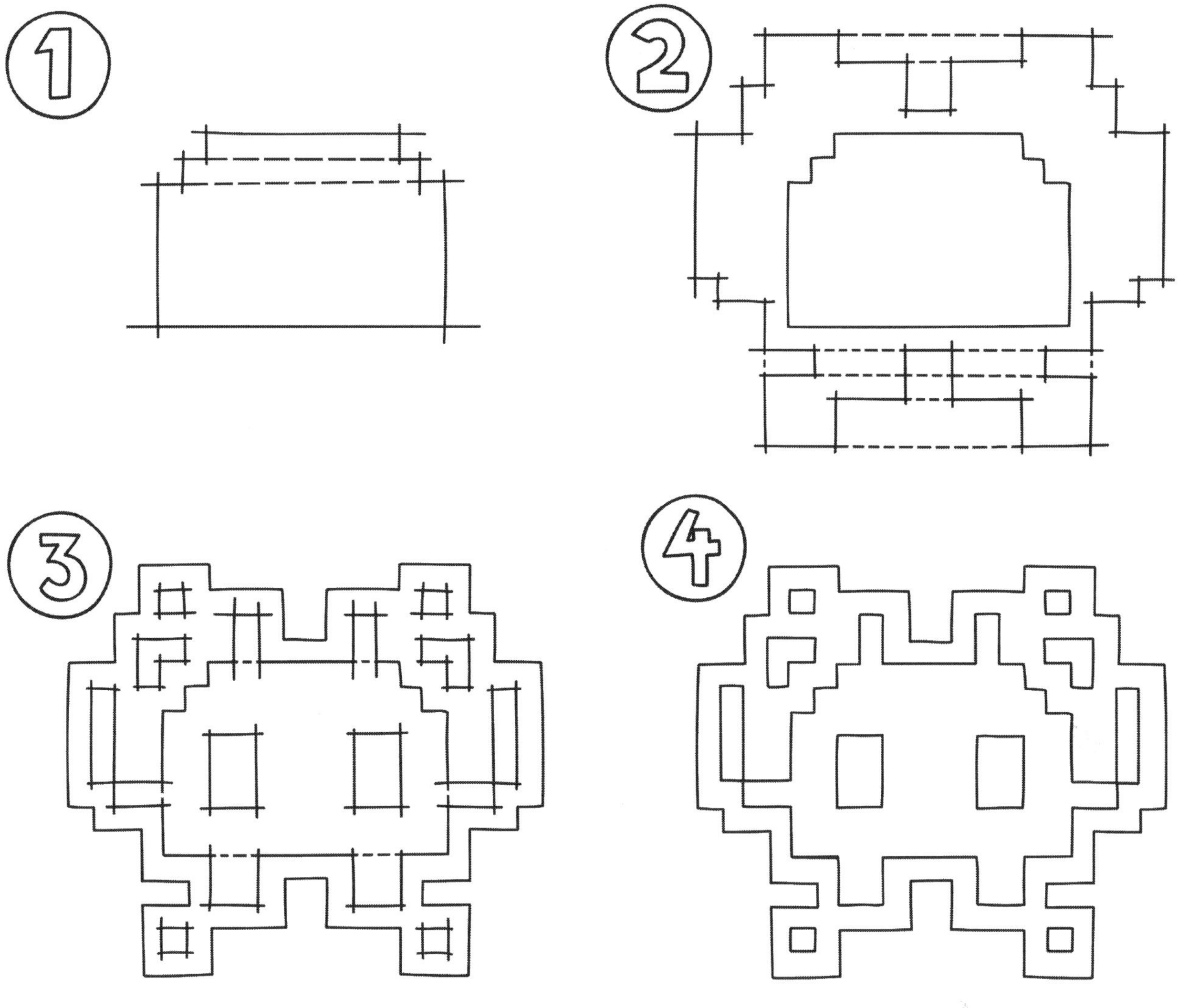

YOU TRY

50

YOU TRY

One last thing - we would love to hear your feedback about this book!

If you found this coloring book enjoyable and useful, we would be very grateful if you posted a short review on Amazon! Your support does make a difference and we read every review personally.

If you would like to leave a review, just head on over to this book's Amazon page and click "Write a customer review".

Thank you for your support!

27317315R00059

Printed in Great Britain
by Amazon